My Journey In Life

Emotional and Inspirational –
Tips the Balanced Scale

Debra Hanna

Vernon House Publishing

The opinions expressed in this manuscript are solely the opinions of the author and do not represent the opinions or thoughts of the publisher. The author has represented and warranted full ownership and/or legal right to publish all the materials in this book.

My Journey In Life
Emotional and Inspirational — Tips the Balanced Scale
All Rights Reserved.
Copyright © 2015 Debra Hanna
v3.0

Cover Photo by: Luiza Lazar. All rights reserved - used with permission.

This book may not be reproduced, transmitted, or stored in whole or in part by any means, including graphic, electronic, or mechanical without the express written consent of the publisher except in the case of brief quotations embodied in critical articles and reviews.

Vernon House Publishing

ISBN: 978-0-578-16131-0

PRINTED IN THE UNITED STATES OF AMERICA

DISCLAIMER:

Dear Readers,
Although this can be considered
a work of non-fiction,
I the author of the content
that can be found here within,
Can assure you, the reader,
That any of the opinions expressed here are my own,
And is a result of the way
in which my mind interprets
A particular situation and or concept.
With this in mind, this book is listed as
a work of fictionalized biography.

Author created: Text, poetry, Illustrations

DEDICATED TO:

Todd

Sandy

Laura

Mike

Shae

Tony

Chris

Tom

WITH SPECIAL THANKS TO:

Todd –
For putting up with me☺

My Mom, Florence Statler -
Who has always inspired me,
Believed in me, and without a doubt,
Knew long before me,
That 1 day my book would come.
So much love for you mom!

Karen Heuter –
This truly wonderful and amazing person
Read into my soul,
And gave me the incentive
To pull out my scraps of paper
From every nook and cranny;
It started with a hat box.

WITH MUCH LOVE AND APPRECIATION
To Mike and Jessica
For the typewriter.
In the end,
That's how my book began.

ALSO,
TO THE DERTZ FAMILY,
FOR MY INSTILLED HUMOR.

ACKNOWLEDGMENTS:

And, a special thanks to —
Maudlin House;
They first published my State Appeal chapter,
Poems, 2, 3, and 4, in their November 2014 issue
         (War and Peace)

My sweet daughter Laura,
Who is my back cover picture photographer.

And... from across the miles,
My heartfelt thanks are for you, Luiza Lazar.
The beauty of your picture titled —
"When autumn leaves start to fall"
    (My front cover picture)
Takes my breath away, and stirs up
The magnificent wonder in me.
        "Together"
     We make my book.

I also dedicate this amazing front cover picture,
to April, my dad, and Chris.
I believe, this is where they eternally reside;
(And why this picture makes me so happy inside)

To everyone out there, as my book speaks for so many;
My raw emotion says it out loud,
Screaming forth... for the happiness, the pain, the reality.
My book is all of us.
We.
This is because of you, that my book is full.
My words are for you.
Thank you.

"All together"
WE, make my book.

FOREWORD:

My 1st husband in 1980
Set every poem I had ever written up in flames.
He didn't want me to write, and proved it.

My 2nd husband in 1992
Allowed our storage facility
To be ripped out from under us, and sold.
For the second time in my life,
My poems are once again gone.

But,
I am finally here today.
To share my feelings —
Short stories in verse I should say.

My thoughts are a little different,
But I hope you can agree —
That's what makes me, me.

MY WRITINGS —
GOOD, BAD, HAPPY OR SAD,
COME FROM MY HEART.
I INVITE YOU ON A JOURNEY WITH ME,
                    LET'S DEPART.

Contents

FISH TALES
1

TAXED
7

SIMPLE RICHES
15, 19, 25

LOVED ONES
32, 38, 42, 46, 49, 50, 52, 54, 56, 59, 61,
65, 69, 71, 74, 77, 79, 82, 85, 89

NIGHT AND DAY
95, 99

ADDICTIONS
104, 107, 109, 112, 120

A DARKER SIDE
127, 130, 132, 135, 138, 143, 149

SHORTIES
157, 159, 161, 162, 164, 166, 169,
170, 173, 176, 178, 180

STATE APPEAL
185, 188, 196, 201

BAD HABITS
209, 213

THE EYES HAVE IT
219

ANGELS ON EARTH
223, 226, 230, 232

DELIVERY
239

DENTAL DEMISE
249

MY BEST FRIEND
255

ILLNESS
259, 263, 264, 267, 269

COLIC
273

SELF WORTH
277, 280, 282, 289, 292

YOUNG LOVE
299, 308

DRIVING W/ ME
314, 315, 317, 319

ABOUT THE AUTHOR
323

FISH TALES

FISH TALES

Our Parrot fish died today.
He was so big and healthy,
I am saddened, shocked, and in dismay.

He was a gift to my boyfriend Todd,
4 years ago on Father's day.

He was called a Bloody Parrot,
All black and red.
He was so tiny and scared,
We didn't think he had much life ahead.

Our other fish are big.
He was intimidated.
We called him scaredy cat.
We would watch him and laugh about that.

Our other fish never bothered him.
He was just scared from within.

Then before we knew it —
It seemed within a day,
He became bigger than the rest of the fish.
Proudly strutting his stuff
When he finally realized this.

The red and black went away.
He turned a bright orange,
Worries no longer coming his way.

He would box the water heater,
I'm surprised it never broke.
We'd hear it smack against the glass,
And knew he was working out.

He was now the Big Cheese, Head Honcho,
Getting bigger by the day.
It was now his pond.

He became a little greedy,
Trying to bully the other fish,
Determined to have his say and his way.

But... He forgot about me in his aggressive plight.
I am the true ruler, the biggest one of all,
And when I saw him being mean —
I would spank him,
And for a while he would be humble once more.

All of my fish have been spanked when they get mean.
1 small tap of my hand and they scram.
I let them know their being bad,
And they instantly agree to behave better for me.

Most think fish just swim in a tank,
But they are my only pets.
My boyfriend doesn't really care for dogs and cats.

So I get personal with them you see,
These fish are my babies and they love me.

They are spoiled chow hounds,
I feed them very well.
I talk to them, play with them,
And people are surprised to see,
How much my fish like to hang out with me.

They laugh when they see me pet them through the glass;
As soon as the fish see my hand,
They rush to me and turn sideways,
Each of them saying... Pet me first please!

They're in a 29 gallon tank; it has become way too small.
We have a 125 gallon tank sitting right next to them,
Almost ready to be done.

Mainly built around our big guys —
Hidden places, so they can go up, down, and through.
An adventure is what they need.
They can no longer have fun
In this little tank indeed.

One morning I woke up, made coffee, fed the fish.
I turn to step away and get started with my day.
A chill went through me; I froze in my steps...
My biggest guy was eating, but he wasn't boisterous.

I sat and watched him for a while.
Eating nice wasn't his style.
40 minutes later I had to go.
He seemed fine and nothing different showed.

When I came home that night,
My eyes went straight to the tank.
I saw all the fish gathered in a corner.
I knew right away something was wrong.
My biggest baby was on the bottom! Upside down!
I freaked out, reached into the tank and picked him up.
He was still breathing and it was hard to face
That his time was up.

I held him upright and petted him for an hour,
Bringing him up for air.
I would relax my hold every so often,
To see if he would swim —
But he couldn't, bringing me to tears again.
Our other fish were so sad.
They kept leaning against my hand while I held him.
They knew I was trying to save him.

Moments later I felt some movement and let him go.
He started to swim!
To the end of the tank and back again.
I said TODD! LOOK! He's swimming!
He's fighting to stay alive!
And Todd said baby — He's fighting for you.
And again I started to cry.
He swam a little longer before he started to sink.
I was right there to get him; my hand never left the tank.

He never made it to his new home.
He was gone soon after that;
And 15 minutes later, he became part of our yard...
Forever.

I finished their tank 7 days later today.
It is beautiful and bittersweet.
He would have been in his glory.
But what I realize,
Is that now his pond is even bigger...
Because he has become
>   Part of Gods story.

TAXED

My boyfriend's Tax man and bookkeeper of 16 years,
Tod, fell sick last year.
We knew something was coming, his look wasn't good.
We tried to get him to go to the doctor,
But he swore — Bad nerves was all he had,
And that everything else was good.
The next we knew,
Tod was rushed to Hines — The V.A. Hospital;
He got there just in time.
We found out he has Liver failure.
He almost didn't make it — He was brought back twice.
He has now been in the hospital for so many months,
We feared for his life.
He couldn't walk or talk anymore,
And we prayed for him to get better.
Above being the tax man,
He was our friend and so much more.

My boyfriend has a Transmission shop,
And his monthly taxes were due on all the parts he used.
Tod had taught me a long time ago
How to do the monthly taxes, so this I know.
It wasn't a big deal to get that out of the way.
But now we overheard on the TV today...
It is Monday, and in 4 days at midnight
The deadline comes —
Taxes better be filed or penalties can abound.
Late or not, if you owe, you owe;
But if a refund was coming, it might not be anymore;

So best not to miss that deadline the TV warned.
We start to panic and realize the bind he's in —
His taxes were not done,
And his tax man wasn't going to be the one.
AND NOW — The bigger problem lurking within...

In dealing with his taxes, his busy bookkeeper
Was 3 years behind, which is allowed by law,
As long as extensions were timely filed.
We immediately start calling tax places
And explain the rush,
That we are in a bind — 4 days until the deadline.
But... no firm wants to quickly do taxes
That are 3 years behind.
I mailed the extension for 2010 — Not too hard.
But, we are on 2007,
And it quickly goes downhill from here.

You need 2006 to complete 2007,
And those copies are still with our tax man so dear.
He had kept them to get ready for the upcoming year.
We call the Hines Hospital — They say...

Tod was released to his sister in Southern Illinois.
She is going to take care of him and see that he gets by.
We don't know her last name or where she lives,
And no tax place will take us without 2006.

Now — This is where I come in and I am truly scared.
Because... I AM DOING MY BOYFRIENDS TAXES
THIS YEAR!

Oh gosh! What a mess! I am so in fear!
He has a home, a business and his personal income!
I have never myself even done
Taxes on my own small job taxed income.
H&R Block was always the tax place for me.
They zip right through and in 11 days have a check for you.
So simple and easy.
But, now I am alone;
And the knowledge to do this I don't own.
Where do I start — How do I begin?
It all looks foreign to me.
My nerves are jumbled and my headache begins.
Then I found his copies from 2005 —
7 forms 10 pages total I realized with a sigh.
I went to the library Monday night,
My hopes not yet taking a dive.
I copied all the 07 forms
And instruction books that I need.
At this point I was feeling a little bit good you see.
I had his old taxes to follow and it showed me
Where lines filled out needed to be.

On Tuesday morning,
Before I could even start filling out forms,
I realized — I had to go through his whole 07 history.
Which wasn't too hard and almost fun.
It didn't take me long to get all those figures done.

By Wednesday morning I was ready to go.
I knew it was going to be hard,
But I hoped not unreasonably so.

The first 2 page form I pulled out, read the instructions,
And with 2005 by my side helping me out,
I'm actually doing this I wanted to shout!

My brain fog is clearing,
And I am almost done, with form 1 page 1.
Then in the middle of form 1 page 2
Right towards the end out of the blue —
I am no longer able to proceed.
The figure to be wrote down next,
Is on another form that hasn't been figured out yet.
I'm thinking that's okay,
I'll put this one to the side and start on the next.
At this point I am still feeling some pride.
The second form is now almost complete,
And I am happy knowing I am getting through this feat.

Then a big buzz kill comes my way.
I cannot finish this form either.
Another one has to be done before I can end this one.
I am going around in circles as you can see;
I cannot complete 1 damn paper.
This is obviously way too big for me.
I feel defeated and can no longer push on today.

Now it is Thursday.
I have every instruction book that I need,
But none of this will help me;
Because the answer I seek is from form 2006 — line 13.
What is his depreciation and amortization amount?
How do I figure this one out?

What does it exactly mean?
How can I figure out numbers that can't be seen..?
You just have to know and I don't know
If you know what I mean.
I pack everything up to take home with me.
6 hours left until the deadline — Midnight tonight.
I am uptight.

Now I am at home.
I keep moving on to other forms,
But not one of them is complete.
Now it is already too late... The deadline was midnight.
Its 1:33am and I am still awake —
There is so much at stake.
I apologize to my guy. He knows how hard I tried.

He says, just let it go and get some sleep now,
Because tomorrow is almost here.
My pillow is full of silent tears.
It pisses me off that I am so close, but can't get there.

Now Friday is here.
I call the Federal numbers begging for help.
Please look up this answer on 2006.
They won't they tell me,
But for a fee they'll send 2006 out to me.
I am a little excited until they say —
4-6 weeks until it gets my way.
I hang up immediately because that wasn't okay;
But they did help me in some way.
They gave me a clue.

Now I am back on those papers struggling through.
I believe I am close to figuring it out.
In fact I think I have it but there is still some doubt.
I check everything again and again.
Then my frowning face turns into a big wide grin.
I have to be right. I feel it from within.
I go with my gut and finish every last paper up.

Then — OH My Gosh — Could it be — Our phone is ringing,
Tod our tax man is on the caller ID!
I snatch the phone up — his voice softly back.
He is on the mend, feeling a lot stronger,
And is worried about us at our end.

I told him of my plight,
And how I missed the deadline last night.
I explained where the problem lied.
He said send it out I think you did fine.
It's not real hard to do.

I said, Tod you have 46 years in the business,
Compared to my 5 days on this road.
I got by with God by my side truth be told.
He said God was by his side too,
That is how he came through;
But his doing taxes has come to an end.
He said his retirement now begins.
I sent my Todd's taxes out that day.

A couple of weeks later a Federal paper came.
My boyfriend says OH! OH! baby,
You did something wrong.
Then he reads... A child credit mistake was made —
They are adding $300 to his refund, is this okay?
Hell yes I say!
Todd says high five me girl you did great.
I'm very proud of you today.
Me too I say.

Simple Richesooo...

SIMPLE RICHES

Face up or face down,
Whether you are happy
Or wearing a frown,
It is always lucky
When a penny is found.
A penny indeed
Is always a blessing.
Don't you see
How easy it would be
To pick up every penny
That there be
Lying on the ground.
It is worth something,
And shouldn't be
So readily
Tossed out and down,
Barely making a sound,
Not being found.
Looks to us
Just like another
Pebble on the ground.

What a travesty!
How fortunate are all we
That we are too rich to care,
About abandoned pennies
Lying everywhere.

None of us
Are too well off
That I can see.

There are so many
Homeless and poor;
With no food for dinner,
No shelter with a door.
Lying helplessly
On the cold ground,
Or a bare floor.

So many kids are hungry,
Their swollen bellies so sad.
Nothing to eat again today.
No nourishment
Coming their way.

And, let's not forget,
About all the abandoned pets
In our world today.
We are over run with strays
That never asked to live this way.
All they did was love us,
And want shelter from the outside;
But instead,
They were kicked to the curb,
No one caring about
How they would survive.

With so many others in need...
The next time you see a penny,
Pick it up please —
Store them in a jar,
And when it's full,
Donate that jar
To a charity.
I guarantee,
Anyone of them
Will benefit from them,
HAPPILY.

You might think
It's not a big deal,
Who cares...?

I can tell you,
All the suffering out there
Dares and hopes
For someone to care.

Then feeling good
Is what you'll be.
Because...
It will help somebody somewhere,
That's a fact.

But you can take it as a dare...
If it will help you to bend down;
Because... That is...
Where it all begins —

On the ground,
Reaching down.
You only have to pick it up you know.
To stoop so low in this way
Is definitely okay;
And the end result will be,
You are picking up those pennies
To help a living thing succeed.
This is one big way
To make a happy heart today.
And all because...
You looked down,
And picked up that penny
That you found.

SIMPLE RICHES

When I was young,
I grew up loving animals and the outside.
Any little critter that came my way,
I would instantly love
And try to bring home every day.
A puppy, a butterfly, crickets, or a snake;
Baby rabbits, frogs, turtles, caterpillars, spiders,
And insects galore.
I thought the fields were great.
Presents everyday awaited me out there.
Nature and I were one.
I could have lived in those fields,
But my mom always made me come home.

My parents would yell
Every time I brought some critter into the house;
But they knew since I was 1,
This is where my happiness comes from.
So when they yelled,
I would look sad for as long as I could;
But my grin was fighting to come out,
Because just a little while longer and I would win out.
That pet would be mine to keep (I silently shout)
Whatever it was, my parents
Learned to let it live in their house.
In a container, box or cage no doubt.
And yes, sometimes they did get out.
The only thing I ever brought home that had to live outside,
Was a cat, my dad didn't like them,
And in our house I could not sneak it by.

He wasn't caring when it came to my pets,
But we had big dogs
That he loved to play and wrestle with.
My mom is an animal lover too.
So — even though she acts stern sometimes,
I don't think she ever really minds.
She just knows what my dad would say,
But I am a Taurus,
And sometimes my stubbornness couldn't be swayed.

We had a litter of puppies at least once a year.
Whenever they got big enough to be given away,
I would cry all day.
We always got to keep 1 of the pups,
But to me that was never enough.

When I grew up, my mom and dad split up.
My mom moved to Tennessee.
What an exciting world it was to me.
She has 80 acres — 50 lands and 30 mountains.
It was the best place yet to pick up pets.

In 1987, my 2 girls and I moved out there for a year.
There was no garbage service out there.
Whatever we couldn't burn
Got carted to the community dump.
It was my daughters and I favorite place to be.
Sounds pretty gross doesn't it?
But not to us you see.
Many of the community people
Dumped their unwanted pets

Into this fenced in yard.
Sometimes there would be only one,
And sometimes, whole litters of puppies
Feeling woe be gone, would be found.
And we would always look around
For the little scared ones — Hidden away.
That dump yard was our pet treasure chest I'd say.

We'd take them all, keep them and care for them,
Until we went to and from Illinois.
Then we'd give them away at rest areas,
To people passing by.
Families that fell in love
With the little ones bouncing around.
Then when they heard how the puppies were found,
Their hearts are bound.
There is a lot of good emotion in this world all around.
It is a wonderful feeling to know,
We've helped lots of puppies find new homes.

I'm grown up enough now to realize
That I can't keep them all,
And that there are so many people out there
Who want and need
This unconditional love that a pet brings.
I still play with spiders, crickets and snakes;
But I have learned to leave them in their natural place.
(The outside environment where they can roam)
That is — Their home.

Todd and I had a mother raccoon
Dig a hole through our roof last year.
Had babies in our attic.
Todd was freaking out.
We finally scared her out.
Turns out she didn't go far;
From our attic to our garage.
The babies' noises sounded cute at first.
They were hiding somewhere in back,
Way up on top;
But eventually their hisses started winning out.
We went camping one weekend,
And when we came back, they were gone.

The end of this story..? I hardly think so.
That was last year,
But this year after the snow, I went into the garage
And saw a big fuzz ball — Its eyes staring at me.
I knew right away it was one of the previous year's babies.
He wasn't mean, he didn't hiss.
I believe he was looking at me with kindness.
I started to talk to him like you would a little baby.
His fat fuzzy face turning side to side.
He got a little closer until I heard Todd's voice outside.
I told him, hurry, go hide,
Todd will freak out if he knows you are back and inside.

I started sneaking food and water to him every day.
He was like my big baby hidden away.
We were growing so close I honestly have to say.
Every chance I had,

I was running into the garage calling for my boy.
Sometimes I would get a little nervous
Thinking he was no longer around;
But then out of nowhere from up above,
I would see him hanging over a ledge peeking at me,
And then he would come down.

One day Todd was going to the garage.
I raced him to the door hoping my big guy was hidden,
But he was waiting for me on the floor,
And, Todd was the one who opened the door!
He screamed when he saw the big boy raccoon,
Slammed the door before I could enter,
Telling me to get in the house.
I said its okay Todd,
And he said no way – Don't you dare – Open that door.
After a while he did calm down,
Called a friend and they walked around
Trying to find how he had gotten in.
Found the hole, boarded it up,
And said from now on the garage stays locked up.
No I said you have to allow him to leave.
We left the garage open until he got out.
Bye bye big boy. I said with a tear in my eye.

Now weeks later he is tearing up our garbage,
And Todd is again freaking out.
I kind of have to smile inside,
Because my big boy is still here and close by.
I realized what I have to do.
I started feeding him again.

Every night behind the garage,
Leaving food and water out;
And the messing around with our garbage cans stopped.

One night with a fire going sitting outside,
Out of the darkness I saw 2 eyes.
The raccoon was right in front of me,
And my smile grew wide.
Hey I say, how is my big big boy.
He cocked his head to the side, listening to every word.
Then I hear Todd come out of the house,
And I say OH! OH! He's coming,
You'd better hurry up and get away.
As if he understood my words — That silly boy jumped,
And in the darkness he was instantly gone.
I still see him and my secret he remains to this day.

Oh look — I see a gardener snake coming out to play,
I think I'll bring him into the house
And watch everyone run away.
Oh my gosh, no way, cancel that —
There is the big gray Jack rabbit, now 2 years old.
I have to run and tell Todd,
This is one big boy he will be happy to see.
We've watched that bunny grow up from a baby.
He likes to hang out with us too.
I just love the fresh air, don't you?

SIMPLE RICHES

I'm plain as day.
Chalk it up to black and white
I'd say.

No frills, no fuss.
Just me,
As how I come.

How nice it would be...
To look like
A sparkling
Perfectly manicured
Well groomed
Well-dressed girl.

But as it is,
This look escapes me.
Something I know for sure.

(What not to wear)
Was the dream team for me.

I always wondered if
They
Could possibly do,
What I have never
Been able to.

But, then again —
Someone like me,
Might be too big of a rough spot
For this group you see;

Because...
Whatever works for others,
Never works for me;
And everything that works for me,
Gets discontinued.
Like I am alone,
In the products I try to own.

I still believe,
I'm an extraordinary girl
In my own way.

I've been smiling
Since the day I was born
That's for sure,
And that's got to mean something,
Don't you concur?

I always greet,
Everyone I pass by and meet.

Matters not to me,
Who they are,
Or what they are about.
A simple smile from me
Gets passed around,
No doubt.

My family vacationed
Once a year,
While I was young.
We traveled everywhere,
And then some.

So...
My smiling face
Has a long history.
I've planted it
All around this world.
So simple and easy.

Simple riches
That comes from me,
I give to everyone out there,
That I see.

An acknowledging smile,
Sent your way —
Simply letting you know,
That someone has thought about you today;

And I spoke to you,
Instead of just looking away,
Which is something
A lot of people do
In this day,
Until they are
Directly confronted
With my big HI.

I surprise a lot of people
In this way;
But, I always get a hello
In return I'd say.

This is my simple riches,
My feel good tool;
And, from me,
To all of you —
I share my smile
With the world.

Loved Ones ♡

I have been through 2 cancer surgeries.
I didn't allow them to put me to sleep.
No shots or medicine would I take.
I didn't know if I could ever get my son away from
His dead beat dad.
My daddy died. A pain I will never get over.
I have an ongoing Thyroid issue,

BUT THIS. . . . .
I WROTE THIS THAT DAY.

TOO MUCH PAIN IN THE WAY.
PAIN THAT. WILL NEVER. GO AWAY.

IT IS INSTILLED IN ME NOW.
THIS I KNOW I CAN SAY.

IT IS BLACK MONDAY.
EVERY MONDAY MORNING. FOREVER + A DAY.

ETERNALLY OUR HEARTS WILL BREAK,
AND OUR EYES WILL BE FILLED WITH TEARS —

WE MISS YOU SO MUCH CHRIS.
WE WISH YOU WERE HERE.
WHY ARN"T YOU HERE?

CHRISTOPHER LEE

39 DAYS SHORT OF HIS 15th BIRTHDAY

LOVED ONES

Chris,
Whenever you were around,
You always looked like the happiest kid in town.
The smile you always wore on your face,
Can never be replaced.
Showing your guts.
Eating with us.
Sleeping with us.
Living with us.
Where are you now?
I can't see you somehow.
Please don't go,
We need you so.
We had no idea you felt so blue.
AND NOW...HOW DO WE GET THROUGH...

WITHOUT YOU!

Without you here with us,
Making a fuss.
OH, CHRIS!
What an end to this!!!
What did we miss???
What had you feeling like this
To bring us to this,
Because now it's you that we miss...
And can't even kiss –
Not one more hug
Can we feel no more.

What is the score...?
I hope God has more.
We will love you Chris, FOREVER AND EVER!
And we will always miss you – EVEN LONGER.

AFTER THIS POEM,
These next few pages are intentionally left blank.

EVEN IF NO ONE SEES OR HEARS. . .

I AM HEAVING —

RIGHT NOW.

RIGHT HERE.

These pages are full of my tears,
And that I only stop here. . .
Because it's hard to breathe —
I miss the shit out of

CHRISTOPHER LEE

It's been almost 2 years now,
And his room still looks the same.

Some people think we are morbid.
But what Todd and I realize —

Is that,
WE WILL NEVER CLEAN HIM OUT OF OUR HOUSE.

His physical being was already pulled from our lives.
His belongings we will cherish.
His memories we will keep alive.

LOVED ONES

Dad,
You are my heart, my life, my soul.
I never said it near enough,
But I hope you know.
In my childish mind
I assumed you would always be here.
I never thought you would go.
I know that nothing lives forever,
But that you wouldn't,
Was something
I didn't know;
And, I'm an adult,
Whose inner child says
Daddy will always be here.
And now I have to smile.

But — You were not always going to be here.
I got a call one day,
That you were in the hospital,
And in a bad way.
I came up to see you
After work that night,
And you gave me a terrible fright,
Because my daddy is not alright.

It was then that I seen
How short life can be.
I don't have any more days with you,
And I can't get back the ones I have missed!

What a twist on my life!
A wrench thrown in this way!
And there was nothing I could do,
I had no say.

I lay my head by you until it was time to go.
I told you I would be back the next day;
And went home crying to Todd,
Telling him that you are not okay.
He held me and said its ok baby.
We'll go and visit him tomorrow.
I knew you were hardly eating or drinking,
But the hospital didn't know,
That Pepsi is the only way you go.

Todd and I came the next day,
With a six pack of Pepsi,
And a little surprise.
Todd said, hey old man,
How would you like an Oscar Mayer Hotdog
Ice cold, right out of the refrigerator?
My dad smiled, opened his eyes wide, shook his head yes,
Ate that hotdog and said...
This was the best food yet.

My dad was way better than yesterday.
We fed him, had a great visit,
And then went home, feeling better about today.

That was the last time I saw my dad alive.
He had a Military burial.
6 guns shot by his side.
Oh how I cried!
My dad who was always so strong,
And never gave in,
Had come to an end.

Dad,
You've had a hard life.
You've worked hard all your life.
This I know;
And because of your ailing,
You quit smoking years ago,
But would still offer me a match,
And to this day,
I still love the smell of that.

You kept 2 cartons of cigarettes
Forever by your side,
And never did you smoke one
Until the day your brother died.

My brothers caught you smoking
At the funeral home outside.

They chastised you badly,
I was so mad inside!
It was not their place to tell you what to do.
They've never smoked a day in their life,
And didn't understand, how right then you needed to.

Your brother just died! Some sympathy, PLEASE!

I just want you to know,
You have always been the truest person,
And my morals will show,
How much you've instilled in me.

You took care of us and provided all that we need.
I have been grown up for years,
And you still took care of me.

I didn't want you to go,
But I didn't want you to remain the same, in pain.

In the last 4 years —
Your breathing was labored,
But still you would stand
And always lend a hand.

You've put up walls in our house,
Fixed our doors,
Serviced our water heater and that's not all —
I know from my brothers and sisters,
You did the same for them.
You gave us your all…
All the way to the end.

I love you Dad,
You were a very fine man.
Amen.

LOVED ONES

Ode to April Williams Cordova,
Before I met you,
Sometimes I would see,
A beautiful girl in flowing skirts,
Strolling her baby around this tree covered Earth.
Here in Tennessee,
With mountains back lighting the scenery.
You were in tune with Mother Nature,
I could see it in your eyes,
In awe of the simplicity,
In a grand scale way.
I've lived here for 2 months,
The day I first met you.
Inside a gas station,
I overheard someone say,
I need some help with my car outside.
I lifted my head, this girl was you.
I'll help you I said,
And you turned to me surprised,
Really?
Yes, let's go outside.
Whatever it was, we figured it out.
You turned to me...
You have a way of knowing things, you said,
You see the aura that surrounds me,
You feel a spiritual connection,
And want us to be friends.
Does this sound crazy to you?
No, I smiled and said.

Right then and there
I left my car in the lot,
Jumped into yours,
And we took off.
The strangest thing is
This didn't seem strange at all,
Like we were old best friends.
Kindred souls you said.
From this 1st day your spirit captured my heart.
You were beautiful, happy and laughed a lot.

Your new born son is Casey Chad,
Your man's named Tom.
You live in the trailer court
Down the road from my moms.
The first time my 2 daughters and I
Came to your house, I was surprised.
Your front door was wide open,
A big smile in your eyes,
You stood there holding Casey,
While 2 puppies bounced by your side.
You took us walking through the woods,
Adorned by a creek.
It's a river, not a creek you said.
We both started laughing.
Simple as that.
You wanted us to help collect things for your basket.
You were making a bouquet.
Come on you said, this is so much fun,
You won't believe what you can find.
Mother Nature is not only beautiful,

She's generous and kind.
We picked the most amazing things,
And you put them together like a cotton candy dream.
This array looked priceless,
Yet it was all free.
Nature's already instilled in me.
Sisters that were meant to be.
Back at your house, we all sat on the floor.
You pulled out your guitar.
We were in awe.
The beauty of your voice,
Your head hanging low,
You pulled from within you,
The depths of your soul.
You wrote all your own songs with God in your heart.
We were moved beyond belief.
Tears streamed down my face.
I felt I had been graced.
You also rocked many well-known songs.
(House of the rising sun) will forever stick with me;
I'll hear you sing it endlessly.
You took us wallowing through mud holes,
Through caves and caverns.

The creek was our swimming pool,
Swinging from a rope, jumping in the water.
Laughing.
The flower child endlessly flitting through the fields —
The beauty of the earth,
The God given bounty,
Ours to feast our senses upon,

Barefoot in the soft moss, and happy.
Endlessly happy.
You are younger than me.
You are younger than me!!!
How can this be?
Your beautiful soul cannot be deceased.
I beg and I plead.
My tornado is freed.
This life I grieve.
Been away too long.
Caught up on it all.
Didn't realize...
This was a final call.
Endless thoughts and words no more.
That is all.
My mind wanders;
Still trying to touch your soul.
Don't even know how to comprehend.
Such a light in my life!
You were my friend.
I'll love you forever man!
This hurts so badly,
But April, I know you are happy in Heaven.
Your giggling soul I feel.
Through my tears, I will try to be happy too.
I know we'll see each other once again.
In Heaven.
Gods home.
Amen.

LOVED ONES

My Aunt Marjie & Uncle Joe,
Met a long time ago.
She was captivated from the start.
Already saw their life planned out.
She was ready to have a family:
But with Joe, his libido was still on the go.
They parted ways and went on with their days:
But the circle of life has a funny way
Of bringing you back
To where you were meant to be –
And, that's what happened
With my Uncle Joe & Aunt Marjorie.
They rekindled their passion,
Their love on the rise.
They looked forward to the future.
Stars in their eyes.
My Aunt Marjie is cute as a pixie, kind and sincere.
I love her red hair,
Silky and straight, like a strawberry blonde.
She was fiery in some ways
But, controlled it well I'd say.
Aunt Marjie, when you and my Uncle Joe got married,
I was so happy for you.
You loved him most your life –
Forever thought, you would need a club,
Like back in the caveman –
Knock him out; drag him to your den.
Life was simple back then.
You knew in your heart, way longer than he,

You and Joe were meant to be;
And, Hot Dang Diddley Dee —
You two got married.
Two hearts intertwined permanently.
You smiled and winked at me ☺
Together ever since,
Life full of struggles and happiness.
Happiness that was meant to be…
The most beautiful family.
Oh, Uncle Joe,
What a toll.

Your Marjie is no longer at home.
God rest her soul.
I know your heart is broken today.
What I can say is…
Be happy for all the beautiful memories,
The smile upon her face.
She's smiling at you from Heaven,
An Angel full of grace.
Mark, Jen, Joe, and Mallorie,
I am sorry you lost your mom,
Such a big part of your family.
But, your mom stayed long enough,
To get you all grown up.
Be proud of who you are today.
She'll live on through you.
She'll never go away.
Aunt Marjorie,
Your pleasantries, have been left on all of we —
Your beautiful smile,

The cutest laugh,
The light in your eyes,
Will now stay steadfast.
Our heart that aches,
Feelings of despair,
But, the light in the skies on this sunny day,
Is the opening of Heaven,
Welcoming your way.
It is Gods way of letting us know,
You are okay.
P.S. Her hair is shoulder length today ☺

LOVED ONES

Pauline, Sharon and Kelly,
I heard your mom died.
I don't remember her well,
But I'm sad on the inside.
I'm sorry for you.
It's something you will never get over.

She went real fast,
And that was best.
She was ready to see her husband at last.
Your dad met her at the gate,
And he wasn't late.
She's happy now,
In the hereafter somehow.

She'll be missed by all,
But take solace in the fact
That she is not sick anymore.
She waited a long time
To again be with your dad.

They are now holding each other and smiling.
They know you are left feeling sad,
But if you could see them together,
I know some how your tears would be glad.

Their happiness is now eternal.
They've reached the Promised Land,
And are forever more
Held in God's hands.
His light will always surround them.

LOVED ONES

My Aunt Darlene was never mean.
A beautiful old fashioned lady
Whose morals were always keen.
I always admired her organized clean house —
How empty it will be now,
Without her moving about.

Dennis, Glen and Jeff —
I am so sorry and I am so sad.
I loved your mom and I loved your dad.
It's devastating that your mom
Is now gone along with your dad.
They're not here anymore and that really sucks!
But your mom is happy up there we have to trust;
Because up there,
Not only do they get to see all those they've missed,
They get to forever watch over us in their eternal bliss.

My memories of Aunt Darlene,
Are mostly when I was young.
Dennis and Glen —
Remember the fun we used to have,
Playing hide and seek at your mom and dads.
Or the time we threw hotdogs around your room —
Your mom walked in on us,
And didn't get over it soon.
We had to climb on the top bunk bed,
That was covered with a net,
And find every last piece of hotdog.

Then we had to clean your room,
While she stood there with a glare
Waiting to hand us the vacuum.

Or Dennis remember the time
We were building Legos on the sidewalk outside?
Your mom came out and acted so proud of us...
Until we lifted the lid,
And she saw that our castle
Was filled with Daddy long legs!

And some of them were just little dots.
Those were the ones that tried to get away,
And you had pulled their legs off,
To ensure their stay.
She was aghast and horrified I'd have to say.
She put her hand over her mouth and looked away.

Our parents, aunts and uncles
Were many and now they are few.
But our cousin status is mighty,
And we are all here for you.

With all of us together we can get through.
Let's lean on each other,
And always remember to give a hug or 2.
We love you Aunt Darlene,
And we thank God for taking care of you.

LOVED ONES

My friend Michelle's grandma,
Was such a beautiful lass.
She rarely ever asked for help,
She prided herself in that.
Though she was getting up in years,
She toiled day-a-lee.
She kept up on her mail and such,
Her carpet runners always angled properly.
She allowed me to vacuum her room,
But always brought her own garbage out.
She'd come down and help me with the dishes,
She was quite the spry little sprout.
She brought love in so many ways —
It's a shame she is no longer here with us today.
She made us laugh, we love her dearly.
The spry grandma sprout is here no more,
But she gave us a lifetime to remember her for.
Her life was long and good in so many ways.
She was with her daughter's family,
Since I can remember way back when,
But God has now chosen her
To come into heaven with him.
Grandma,
In our hearts you were always the bell of the ball.
We will miss you so dearly
Each and every day,
I don't believe our sadness will ever go away.
Grandma,

We are not sure
Why you could not stay;
But we are so happy to have you,
For as long as we did.
We will love you and remember you always.
In us you will always live.
You are in heaven now,
Happy, healthy, and no longer in harm's way.
God speed grandma,
Because now we know
You are okay.

LOVED ONES

My cousin Larry,
Was always the happiest guy.
He made everyone laugh so hard,
Till we had tears running out of our eyes.
Like a big ole marshmallow of sticky goodness,
He left a piece of him
On every man, woman and child,
That has ever had the delight,
To have met him in life.
Who could ever forget this big hearted guy —?
The impish grin that marked his face,
Is the memory that I will remember,
As he rests in peace.
Larry never came out of his sickness,
And that's how I can understand,
Why he was taken from us —
God didn't want any more suffering for this man.
Larry was always so happy and full of life.
It didn't seem fair
For him to live in a hospital bed —
Never again to enjoy anything nice.
Death then seems eminent,
When life no longer feels real.
So — The best thing I can say about Larry today —
His hospital bed was kicked to the curb.
He did it himself,
Like Hercules I heard.
No longer is he feeling alone and in pain.
With his new wings and rollerblades,

He is now skating on Gods terrain.
His mom, dad, aunts and uncles
That have gone —
Are now embracing him;
And with a kiss on the head from his mom,
His impish grin comes forth
And again abounds.
In Gods heaven he is healthy.
He can see us. And I believe he is happy now.
Just look at the twinkling in the stars —
His grinning out there — Looms large.

LOVED ONES

Mr. Kenneth Miller,
With the Kia Sedona.
I feel we've known you
A big part of our lives,
And recently you told Todd
You were thinking of a new ride.
Todd said, you do what you need to,
But he had a strange feeling inside.
He hoped you lived long enough
To enjoy this new ride.
You are energetic and spry.
Humble and kind.
In perseverance, you have clout.
A wonderful mentor.
You shared your knowledge
Throughout your life,
Helping everyone learn
All that is right.
You were selfless
In this plight.
It's what you were born to do.
Your life's work
Already planned for you.
The many accolades' behind you
Prove this is so.
A man, who is true blue.
I proudly say this of you.
Always a smile upon your face,
The gentlest of human race.

You enjoyed your new ride.
I can't say for how long,
Because, all too soon
Your time had come.
You were 88 years young.
Mr. Ken is now in the heavenly skies.
He lived a good life whilst he was alive.
He touched our hearts,
We are grateful inside,
To have known this longevity guy.
And, as sad as many of us
Will always be...
Well, his Delores was waiting for him.
She snatched him up instantly.
They are now holding hands and smiling.
For all eternity.
Their everlasting love
Grows on, in Gods sanctuary.
And, I have no doubt
He'll forever watch over you all...
His heart stretches
Far past the stars.
And, his Cheshire grins?
Well, the Moon can no longer compete.
It is now called – Kens smile,
And every time you look into the sky,
He'll be smiling across the miles ...
Like a rainbow that has
No beginning or end,
His smile is there for you to see,
Endlessly moving,

But staying in view,
For he so loved all of you!
And behind our tears, a smile will shine,
Because your memories
We'll cherish a life time.
We love you Mr. Kenneth Miller.
You were the man of your time.
Thank you for being in all our lives.
Amen

LOVED ONES

Bonnie — Your Grandmother has passed.
What a sad day it is,
That she is no longer here.
But let us feel blessed
For the long life that she had.
Now her aches and pains have subsided at last.
And for the first time in so many years…
Grandma can now again see
All those so dear.
The ones she'd already lost
Are now near.

And us — ?
We are even closer.
Looking through that big Kaleidoscope
From the heavens in the sky,
More so than she ever could —
Lying in a bed,
Watching the hours tick by.

She can now see us all the time,
And I'm sure grandma can't help,
But to send smiles your way.
You loved her, always visited her,
And she knows that you were thankful for her
In every way.

In heaven she now knits a white pillow case.
Dark clouds have seen their day.

She doesn't want you to be sad,
And she knows you are,
Because she is gone.

But her suffering has passed —
She is not forlorn.

So — don't be too blue.
Grandma is now with God,
And he knows just what to do.

For her, eternity is now
So warm and light.
I don't believe in heaven
It is ever a dark night.

She is no longer stuck in a small room.
She has come to fruition —
An angel — Now in full bloom.

Happy and smiling,
The sun shines down on us today.
It is her way of letting us know she is ok.

We love you grandma,
We wish you everlasting peace on this day.

LOVED ONES

Cassie —
Your Danny died.
2 days after his son was born.
A sad way to bring in this little one.
What a horrible shock..?..?
It is hard to believe that he is gone.
How could this be?
He just added a son
To his growing family.
There were no warnings —
No signs.
He was happy that day.
You Cassie were coming home from the hospital,
Where his new child still lays.
He was concerned about his son;
But the doctor said,
He'll be ok,
And soon he can come home.

What went awry?
Why God... Did you right then
Need Dan back by your side...?

His babies are all so young,
And Dan was the only dad,
That Mikey had really known;
And Cassie — A beautiful girl,
With a heart full of gold —
Loved Danny so.

Through her,
He learned to be bold.
Life had given him so much meaning,
When Cassie introduced herself to him,
And changed him — 10 fold.
He was so happy —
Proud of his new wife.
With her and her son,
Dan never thought twice.
I believe this was the first time,
He thanked God for his life.
This really sucks!
Why was Dan taken from us?
He was still so young —
Just starting to come into his prime,
Finally getting a grip on life;
And now —
Life has passed him by..?
Why???
Why aren't we let in on the why?
Because right now,
Only God knows why;
And now all we can do is cry and sigh —
Because our understanding won't comply.

Dan was a hardworking man,
Who struggled for his family.
He was giving them his all,
And wasn't ever going to let them fall.

What a cruel surprise to us all —
Now our hearts are stuck —
In a drifting abandoned boat —
For we can't ever bring him back —
Reality has spoken, like a slap —
While all of our voices
Are lost in our throats;
We are still in shock.
The blood drains from our empty face —
We cannot quite comprehend what has taken place...
Was it a heart attack?
Or a hidden Aneurysm that broke open wide...
Our mind is in re — wined.
We don't understand what happened.
Not this time.

This causes our thoughts to endlessly race.
We can spend the rest of our lives
Guessing and wondering why.
But will we ever know for sure?
Years from now,
That thought will ebb slightly from our mind.

But we do know —
Dan is now in the endless boundaries of Heaven.
Gods home.
And you know what?
Whatever the reason be —
God brought him back fast.
He wasn't meant to suffer in endless pain —
That wasn't his path.

Cassie, what I am thankful for —
Is you.
If Dan had still been alone with his mom
When she died —
I don't know what would have become of him.
His aloneness would of grew.
But that's not what happened.
Because Cassie, he met you.
Through you Cassie — He was able to achieve
What life is all about.
I know there is so much sadness in your heart;
But you can also be happy,
Because alone, he did not depart.
He left a whole family of hearts.

A part of him — we'll always — get to see.
He lived long enough
To have his own family;
And that brings forth a smile from within.

There weren't many pictures
Of Dan in life;
But he is branded into our memories —
FOREVER.
The guy who was never anything but nice.

Cassie, Mike, Lilly and little Tom,
I am so sorry that Dan, your dad is gone.

Dan is now in heaven on this December day.
And — even if we don't understand...
It is God's chosen path
We must follow in the end.

LOVED ONES

Darlene suffered from the time she was young.
She was just a teenager,
When her Thyroid was done.
Then Cancer came out,
And attacked her about.
Though her body kept suffering,
Her heart did not.

She was beautiful and pleasant,
Slender and elegant.
The look of Royalty.
Darlene should be
The name of a Queen;
Except she is not haughty,
Not once ever mean.

For a few years
She was on the mend,
Trying to stay positive...

But then,
The illness came back,
And attacked her again.

She somehow knew
That she was close to being done —

But she kept
Hanging in there,
Her will
Carrying her on.

Another Battle —
Fought yet again.

She came out ahead,
But the Demons not gone.

Recovery is short.

Sadly...

Darlene's time has come.

At 48 years young.

Her sun is now
The Heavenly skies,
And Darlene is free
Of all that was ailing.
She rests peacefully.

But you Kevin,
With your own
Problems at hand.
You've been dealt a lot yourself —
Been taken down a peg.

Though nothing
Seemed to matter,
When you held
Darlene's hand.

Your Darlene is now gone,
And even if you knew
Of this life's plan —
It doesn't make it
Any easier...
When someone you love
Comes to an end.

How devastating man!

I know your heart is now aching.
Your sadness is boss;
But you've had
A wonderful life together,
All is not lost.
Something that many people
Never get to achieve —
You were able to have with Darlene.

You both vacationed and traveled,
You both stayed at home.
You both played w/ your dog,
Your hearts were as one.
Her time was cut short,
But true happiness was found.
You were her King,
And for her...
You'd kiss the ground.
You found a soul mate.
A deal that's gone right.
Someone you can cherish,

And someone...
Who gave back to you.
So very nice.

Butterflies now seem so rare;
But when I heard of Darlene's passing —

Well...
I now see butterflies everywhere.
I think she is showing us
Her new wings,
And like the beautiful Butterfly —
She floats gracefully by.
She has no sickness,
She has no disease.
She is high in the sky,
And free...
For all eternity.

So Kevin,
The next time you see
A beautiful butterfly —
Know that Darlene is still here,
And she's showing you
She's thinking about you,
But also...
She's doing just fine.

Think of the beautiful memories,
And be happy my friend —
Because the life line of Darlene,
Was yours to the end.

LOVED ONES

George,
I am so sorry that your son is gone.
When I found out —
I crumpled to the floor.
Devastation overpowering me.
Tears flooded my eyes,
And I could see no more.
Emotions so raw.
What you have endured.
The most agonizing heartache
Of all this Earth.
There are no words to console you.
One would almost think
No hope can be brought
When you are so
Devastatingly sickened in your heart.
Our tears will blend forever.
One and the same.
A loss —
That can never
Be regained.
A child —
Who will forever remain.
There isn't hope,
But there is an easiness of thought;
What couldn't happen
Here on Earth...
Will happen up there ^
With God.

And if God believes
With him
Your son was meant to be —
He knows something we don't.
Too hard for us to see;
But he is the all knowing
Of what needs to be.
He saved your son from future harm.
This I have to believe.
It's the only light I see.
I'm sorry George. Truly.

LOVED ONES

Mr. Houle…
A great prominent man,
Spent his life achieving all that he can.
His wife Marilyn he adored.
So very long ago she stole his heart.
Together ever since.
Now on the verge of their 50th.
Way to go, high five to you both!
A long life together
Is something to boast.
They owned and ran Rosewood West.
A restaurant and banquet facility
On the corner of Cal-sag.
A booming business made possible
By the lengthy hours of this families hands.
Mr. Houle was quite the man.
Direct, outgoing, and strong.
His author ITive personality
Might have scared some,
But the smile he wore,
Showed he was human.
A real go getter since back in the day,
He could have been Mayor
I heard people say;
But being worn out with unpleasentries
Was not his plight.
Creating a following in fine dining
Was his triple A score.
The excellent meals,

The prime cuts of meat,
The fresh fish and shrimp,
A well-stocked bar;
This beautiful facility they owned,
Was the main attraction
For miles around.
They brought life to this area and town.
Marilyn, Michael, Patrick, Joey, Zach and Chase,
Your husband, your dad, and your paw is now gone.
I feel sorry and forlorn.
He lived a good life,
While he put up a good fight;
And I don't believe his fight was gone —

His will could have forever carried him on.
His body just couldn't last as long.
No regrets Mike,
You did all you could.
You've always been there for your dad,
Even in moments that weren't so good.
In the last years
When your dads' health started to decline,
You pushed him because you loved him,
And even if you weren't always kind,
Your dad understood you.
Michael —
You have his soul and mind.
You are two of a kind.
I think this is super fine.
You took care of your dad
All the way to the end,

And now your dad is watching you from heaven.
Smiling and proud as all hell of you man!
Know you done right my friend.
Lastly I have to say,
Mr. David Houle
Was mostly in a bed.
He didn't get to run around anymore,
His thoughts... mostly wandered instead.
He was a stand up, go to guy.
Powerful, alive, and full of pride...
His last few years of suffering couldn't last —
It was a dead end path.
He had to have release from that,
And you can't ask for more
Than to be taken out fast —
No time to think,
No time to react,
No time to suffer,
Instantly on a new path.
Heaven.
Where there is no sadness.
We are the only ones with sadness.
Us — left behind;
But up there with God,
He is just fine.
He is again in his prime.
For all the rest of time.

LOVED ONES

Cathy, a beautiful girl,
With hair like Cinderella.
You were always nice to me,
And I appreciate that greatly.
What happened Cathy..?
What went wrong?
On the inside
You were sick,
But where
Did the massive heart attack
Come from?
I'm truly shocked.
I can't believe you are gone.
How unexpected
When you weren't yet so old.
Shows me,
That you never quite know –
That you don't always have the time
To right the wrongs –
To lay your heart on the line –
To get in touch with everyone
And say –
I love you,
Or I miss you.
I thought of you.
You made me smile today.
And, you and me Cathy,
Well, we didn't see each other much.
Sad to say...

It seems to be,
When my mom and dad split up,
The family all stopped hanging out.
So...
Now wakes seem to be
Our gathering place these days;
And it wasn't that long,
Since I saw you last.
You looked normal and healthy.
It was your husband, my cousin
That had all the problems, I believe.
He is still trying to recoup
From all the past ailing.
You were there for him,
Helping him come along.
I think no one knew
Your ailing would be the end of you.
So abruptly...
POOF!
Just like that
You were gone.
And sadly Cathy
We will now gather again.
This side of the coffin —
Looking a little small.
I'm sorry Cathy,
Sad to see you go.
Wish more of you
I would have got to know.
But, no matter if we're seen
Few and far in-between —

The camaraderie is still here.
We are all related,
Our hearts intertwined
For this families life line.
Some of us great.
Some of us good.
Some of us sad.
Some of us misunderstood.
It matters not,
Which area we fall in,
For we are all kin;
And we'll always be here for each other,
Until the end.
Cathy,
You've now reached an end to this life...
But a new beginning awaits
In Gods paradise.
Ailments subside...
You are now an Angel.
Forever flying high.

LOVED ONES

Oh Kenny,
1st your mom, and now your dad?
How devastating, awful and sad.
You haven't yet healed from your mom,
And now your dad has passed along.
My heart hurts for you.
I know you are forlorn.
Your heart has been ripped up and torn.
The 2 people you loved the most are gone.
But, now they are happy and healthy Kenny —
And, smiling at you from above…
You have all their love!
They'll be with you always…
They're here with you right now!
They'll help you get through this somehow.
I know you now face
A big change in your life…
This big loss,
And the new direction
That lies in wait —
The new beginning,
You have to take.
I don't know
What you are going to do,
Or how it is going to go,
But you can do this Kenny.
This I know.
Allow yourself the time you need.
No rash decisions.

Relax for a while.
Lie back and breathe.
It will come to you eventually,
And, when it does...
This new door will open suddenly —
Maybe not a miracle,
But a reason to be here.
A reason to believe and go on
That's for sure.
You are still needed Kenny.
Hang in there. I am so sorry for your hurt.

LOVED ONES

Mrs. Hoehn,
I'm sorry you had to go in the cold.

The sun always kept you warm
Vibrant and bold.

You'd bask in the rays,
Then bustle and go.
The care you took of your family,
Leaves me feeling aglow.

You were stern in your opinion,
But loved everyone so.

You treated everyone equally;
Although grandchildren
Took center stage in your heart.

You taught me many things
That I've not forgot.

From my troublesome marriage,
To my colicky babe,

You and Chuck were always here for us.
I love you like my family,
Still today.

Ma and pa,
Most of all,
I remember the video tapes
You sent to my girls
From the time they were small.

You'd both be singing Merry Christmas
Or happy birthday,
While grandpa's arms swung along.
You were the highlight
Of all the cartoons
That was to come.

Every day I put grandma & grandpa
On the TV;
Rewinding it over and over again.
You made my girls happy.
Including me.

I know now
You are happy as can be.
Swimming in Gods heaven
The everlasting sanctuary.

Chuck is again by your side.
He is having his 1 a day whiskey sour,
And I know you're scolding him
With love in your eyes.

You will shine down on the rest of us.
Forever more.
From you and pa,
This I do believe.
I am happy to have been
A part of thee.

LOVED ONES

Debi,
I talked to my mom on Mother's Day,
And didn't know,
That you had talked to her also.
I was surprised —
But I was also sorry to hear
About your Cancer demise.
It brings tears to my eyes.

The last time I saw you,
You were proud to have hair so long —
I know how you feel
Now that it's gone.
We are both like Sampson,
Our hair is our strength.
Your hair will grow back,
And mine doesn't grow,
But with the strength of us in each other —
We will always be bold.

So listen to me...
With a cute face like that,
There is no doubt,
If you are sporting a pixie,
It is a matter of fact
That you can carry that!

You were my best friend,
Since I can remember,

Way back when.
We've had way more ups than downs,
You were always the sexy one,
And I was always the clown.

Our fights were rare,
But our stubbornness was always there.

Even if we were not talking,
We always did when Robbie's birthday was here;
And so many years ago,
The last time I had called —
Your number was gone.
I couldn't bear to miss Robbie's day,
So I called The Broken Yolk —
You haven't been there in a year they said.
What dismay.
I have missed you and it seems
Like forever + a day,
Since I've seen your terrific smile
Come my way.

Breaking the tradition of Robbie's day —
That was something,
Just between me and you,
That started out by accident,
And then every year
Stayed true blue.

Just so you know,
Every year on his day —

In my heart and out loud I would say,
Happy Birthday Robbie,
We love you.
We sure are missing you today...

So if my mom has your address,
This I will send —
Otherwise it goes back in my book,
To the chapter I keep alive,
Because to me it has no end.
I Love you Deb.
You'll always be my friend.

LOVED ONES

Fayez was the greatest grandpa I ever knew.
Took care of his grandchildren,
Like only a grandpa could do.
He did everything for them and with them
From the time they were born.
His gentle, kind, caring ways
The children adored.
Mariam, Ziyad, Yazmeen and the other little guys
Were the light in his eyes —
The sparkle in his thoughts —
The lift in his steps —
The beating of his heart.
His closest ties — from them
He was never far apart.
They never wanted for anything,
Because grandpa was around.
Picking them up.
Taking them on trips.
Overnight stays.
Yay! Grandpa is here again today!
Hurry mom — get us dressed fast.
It's a race to see who gets to his car first,
And grandpa would smile and say — Silly kids...
You are all number 1 in my book.
Grandpa was the man;
And now somehow these little hearts
Will have to try to comprehend and understand,
That grandpa is now in heaven.
He can no longer pick them up

Or hang out for the day;
But he will forever watch over them.
I know he'll keep harm from their way.
His duties as grandpa
Will live long past this day,
For an eternity his spirit will guide their way.
Aladdin and Laura, Ramsi and Rami.
Don't know what to say.
Your beloved father, your best friend
Is no longer here today.

No one was ready for this.
The feeling of shock and forlorn for this gentle man
Who cared for everyone.
He looked down on no one,
And always extended his home or his hand.
Not an inkling,
Not a knowhow,
So alive and pleasant.
Then taken out the same day.
His lively happiness now drumming through our mind...
It seemed only hours ago that he was fine —
Still making plans,
He planned all the time.
I believe, the smile he wore on his face
When he was found,
Was also a plan...
He loved everyone as only he can.
I believe it was his thought of all of you
That made him smile in the end.

He left showing you
How much love is still instilled in him.
He left us the meaning of happiness man!
And we must absorb this,
And do for him,
To give back to this selfless man —
Our father, our grandpa, our very best friend.
I think we should all give Fayez
A cheering high five!
For he lived his life being all that he can for us
Whilst he was alive;
And even in the suddenness of his passing by...
He left his smile for us
To always carry inside.
We love you Cedo.
Not a day will go by
Without us thinking about you.
You will never be forgotten.
This day marks your eternal life in heaven and
The heaviness in our hearts will ebb but never pass by.
The meaning of you will forever live within us.
God bless and thank you, for being in all of our lives.

Beautiful Baby Zachary

Fought hard
For 19 days —

His existence
Was given less than 5

LOVED ONES

A baby is a gift from God
That comes our way.
We are over joyed and we pray
That everything is okay.

More often than not
This is true;
And, our little one is wrapped in pink or blue.

But sometimes – sometimes
Something is not right.
There is no rhyme or reason.
Just an unimaginable why.
We feel sick and faint and devastated and far away...
HOW could this of possibly happened
To my little one today!
We will spend forever wondering why, I'm sad to say.

But, God only gives what we can take;
And the specialist baby of all,
Is the one we don't get to physically keep.
Zachary is here for a bigger reason.
His stay is short and bittersweet.

All of our hearts swelled 100x's bigger this day.
We are so full of emotion and don't know what to say...
How to think, do I feel – will I never not feel...
Is. This. Really. Real..?

Why is my child not here today???
I am begging you Lord,
I cannot handle that he didn't stay!!!

Your life is not easy, I think God would say.
I brought this little one to you
To shed light on your day.

To renew your love, your emotion, your virtue,
Your family camaraderie —
Take nothing at face value!

Your hearts became one when Zachary was born.
I know you are forlorn;
But, all of the inner reasons for why we are here,
Are now at the surface — Hold on to them dear.

How can we go throughout life so disgruntled
And let discontentment come our way,
When little Zachary struggled
Just to breathe and stay alive!
There is a meaning in all of this
That we cannot hide, and have to abide.

In some twisted way...
We feel an eternity has passed,
When actuality is mere days.

Zachary was chosen to be here for just a short while.
But, we were given the opportunity to love him, to hold him,
And that thought, deserves a smile.

We'll bless Zachary and then let God take him home.
Great Grandma is already smiling.
Her thoughts are of eternal spoiling;
And you can't chastise her; she is too far away —
But between Great Grandma and God —
Please know that your little one is okay.

Gina, Shawn and Matt, my heart goes out to you today.
Your son and your brother couldn't stay
Here on earth in the way that we liked.
His body didn't last, but his heart will forever in ours.
You are the only mother, father and big brother,
That he will ever have.
Always be glad,
You were chosen in this way.

Matt I know you are a sad boy today,
Because your brother didn't stay.
But, Zach knows how much you love him,
And maybe one day — you will again have a sibling
With whom you can love and play;
Then you and Zachary will both be big brothers,
One of the earths and one of the skies —
And, Zach will always be here for you on the inside.

Happiness for Zachary's birth, sadness for his loss.
All at the same time — let us intertwine
Our arms and our hearts.

God now needs Zachary back by his side.

Let us pray for this little one today.
Let our hearts be filled with pride,
For we got to know this important little guy;
Staying here longer than anyone ever thought he could,
His heart and soul is everything that is good.

Let us show him the courage he showed us.
To go beyond the limit —
Let us show the strength that he showed us.
To mend broken thoughts —
Let us show the compassion he showed us.
To love endlessly — Let's show him the heart he gave us.
Let us show Zachary pleasure in that we had by his stay.

Zachary, you will forever remain in our hearts and souls
For an eternity + a day.
You have made us all a better person,
Each in our own way.
We love you Zachary, sleep peacefully.
You've had a rough stay.
Now you are healthy in heaven;
And, this thought gives us our smile
On this sad day.

Night & Day

NIGHT AND DAY —
The Nightmare

I never let others touch my hair;
Because it seems to me
They really don't listen
To what I say.
They hack off so many inches,
Leaving none to spare;
And just because they do it professionally,
They feel they've a right to,
Like it's okay,
As if we shouldn't care —
Even if we didn't want short hair.
I am scissors shy,
And Beauticians haven't got a clue…
If I could carry a gun,
That's what I would do.
Feeling threatened I would pull it out
And then turn that threat on you!
I know that this would guarantee
Getting the trim that ought to be.
Yes, we all know guns are not allowed
So I can't shoot to kill —
But I can dodge the Beautician bullet,
And I definitely will.
I do everything myself,
And it's not half bad.
I may not be a professional,
But long hair — is what I still have.

Then one day highlighting hair
Came out in the biggest way.
It looks so cool that I'd have to say,
I broke out of my shell
And took off work for a ½ of day.
I ran to my appointment, happy all the way.
No cut for me,
Just some color is all I need.
And that is all it will be.
I thought happily.
The first warning bell to go off in me…
Is when she pulled out a cap.
No foils to be seen.
Okay I can deal with that, I thought nervously.

When she was done I guess I looked ok.
My hair didn't match the thought in my head,
But, I had made it through the day.
Then she suggested a little trim.
My hair began to stand on end…
NO WAY! I told her over and over again.
She said your ends are damaged,
Your hair is not growing properly.
Please – let me cut just a little bit
And then you will see
How much longer and healthier your hair will be.
I didn't want to give in,
But she did talk me into that little trim.
She showed me only bare edges were falling to the floor.
I got comfortable – and then,
SHE DID ME IN!

She cut bare edges alright.
Over and over it seemed to me;
And when she was done,
She turned me around — And I SCREAMED!
WANTING SO BAD TO CHOKE HER SOME.
My hair that was almost to my elbows…
Is now shoulder length.
I felt like I was going to pass out.
Feeling dizzy, faint, out of strength.
How could she do this to me??
I had told her my Sampson story.
She then showed me, a picture of her hubby and her.
They both have the longest hair.
She then assured me she was someone who really cares
And wouldn't dare cut off my hair.
And now, I am left with nightmares!
This is the worst thing that could happen to me.
I was 41 at the time feeling good in my prime.
BUT —
Her major hair cut stunted my hair growth;
And to this day…
6 years later I want to make her pay!
Because my hair is still shoulder length today.
How dare her have the balls to have done me this way!
I dream about going into her shop
And hacking her hair away — then shaving her bald!
How happy then would that long haired bitch be?
When she is more hairless than me.

Summation:
I could cry a thousand tears.
It wouldn't be enough.
I could cry until every last drop of water
Evaporated from my body.
It wouldn't be enough.
You can't replace what was cut.
Stuck in a depressed rut.
An endless sentence.
I'm so f**ked up.
I was on top of the mountain.
I got pushed off.
I managed to save myself,
But, my flowing hair took the brunt.
Rapunzel now I am not.
Still in shock.
My strength is gone.
My heart is lost.
All because,
This bitch cut over a foot off.
Evil thoughts.
Cheshire grins.
In my own mind,
I've already retaliated.
She's lucky I'm human.
I kept my monster inside.
Some people can't do that.
She's lucky.
This time.

NIGHT AND DAY —
The Sun

My stepson's girlfriend
Is such a great girl.
She's opening up her own Hair Salon,
And at 25,
She is on top of the world.
I'm so proud of her,
And happy as can be.
What good fortune to come her way.
She's doing right by God,
And this I know I can say.
She has all the right focus,
And plenty of drive —
Her up dos are phenomenal,
And her highlighting is so fine.
As for cutting hair,
She is so there.
Need a dye job?
Jess is a color expert,
And that might not seem rare,
But she takes semi-annual classes
To ensure that she constantly learns
All the latest about hair.
She keeps herself updated,
That's a fact.
Her beautiful personality draws you in,
And when she's done working on you,
You know it's a win-win situation for you;

And, from then on out,
No one else will ever do.
Everyone loves Jessica,
Because her style can't be beat.
So — we'll renovate this ole building
That has been empty for a year.
It looks like hell,
But with total content cleaning,
From the floor to the ceiling,
Then a little bit of the lipstick and rouge
We know so well,
This place will easily be looking swell.

We'll rip out the carpeting, lay some new.
The walls will get painted and when we're through,
We'll sand the wood floors and stain them too.
Then, we'll put down new tile, only skid resistant will do.
We'll work our fingers to the bone,
And when we are done —
Jessica's baby will be born.
(Always Hair) is the name she picked.
The shop opens May 29, 2010.
We are so excited about it.
So here's to you Mike and Jessica,
Let's have a Champagne toast —
Your doors will soon be open,
And we are so very proud of you both.

Addictions

My son lived with his dead beat dad...
He was introduced to the needle.
Eventually —
Got busted with his dad,
The marks obvious on both of their arms —
Took Tony away,
And for a year he became a ward of the state,
In a drug Rehabilitation Center.

It has been almost a year now since Tony's been out.
He sees now —
What he thought was living, was actually the living dead.
He feels again what life is truly about;
And we are very happy and thankful no doubt.
He's back with all of us, who truly love him,
And I am on my knees
Thanking God for watching over him.
Soon he'll be turning 19 —
What a great way to begin this endless path of life,
And it's hopes and dreams.
Now life through his eyes finally gets to be seen.

I love you Anthony.
I thank you for not giving up,
And I thank you for moving forward.

Many years later, I have to add;
Tony and Toms dad has mellowed.
He too got away from dismay.
Their relationship is decent today.

ADDICTIONS

Hey Hey Tony,
Don't be blue.
You know I love you,
And I'm here for you.
I may have not always been there
In the best of ways,
But my heart has never strayed.

I'm happy for you right now,
Even if you are not.
If you hadn't had this intervention,
You would have fallen apart.

You are too young
To have done so much.
Your body is resilient,
But only for so long.
The drugs and lifestyle
We're going to catch up to you
And start to shut you down.

I need to see you grow up,
And live a healthy life.
I would love in the future
To come to your house and visit,
Meet your new wife,
See you have a baby or 2,
A dog sure would be nice.
Just to know you are truly enjoying your life.

I know this is in the future,
And you might not see it right now,
But the chance you've been given
To head down a new path,
Comforts me in knowing how,
You can be what you were meant to be.

An intelligent young man,
Who people are going to look up to and see,
That you made your way,
And you are standing tall and proud today.
So wash the mud off your feet.
Start stepping to a new beat.
The road has been long,
And it's not over being hard,
But things will get easier,
When you get used to a normal life.
Working and earning your money,
Socializing and paying your way,
Will put a smile on your face,
And make you happier,
More and more every day.

A deadbeat life will no longer give you sad thoughts.
Now your hope can be lifted up.
An apartment, a job, a car and a girlfriend or 2,
What man wouldn't be happy with that?
I ask of you.

I know it is very hard right now
At this very moment.

But I swear on my life,
And I promise you this —
Years from now you'll look back on your life,
And be glad you went through this.
Do you know why?
Because not only will you be happy on the outside,
Your feelings and thoughts
Will also be happy on the inside.

When you truly feel good about yourself
And what you are doing —
You'll be unstoppable.

You were the child I'd always longed for,
And it wasn't so you'd lie down and die.
It was for you to soar way up high!

You have people to meet,
And places to go,
Don't be too slow.
The world is waiting for you,
And when you go,
You are going to be in style, I know.
I love you my son. I wanted YOU to know.

ADDICTIONS

Hey Tony,
How are you?
Not much going on,
Just writing to say I LOVE YOU!
Same ole stuff, different day.

Do you wonder sometimes..?
If things will ever go our way?

I definitely get dismayed now and then too.
But the bright spot is ...
Time is forever changing,
Always bringing our hope anew.
Sometimes you have to stir up the stagnant pond
And, filter out the goo.
Because change is always eminent.
This is what keeps us alive and new.

So here's to today and tomorrow.
You will get passed this.
I'd bet my last dollar.
Every day might seem the same,
But it changes with the sun and the moon.
And, one day we'll break through and see,
Every day is special too.

When life has meaning, you feel the best.
But not many realize how much of life is left.
You may feel so old, when you are so young,

But, there is a million years of life left
To learn about son.
The day is actually never done.

We sleep to rest and rejuvenate our bods,
Then wake up to life that is out there
STRETCHING FAR —
Far beyond the eye can see —
It is out there,
And, it is out there for you and me.

Life is a great place to be.
When you think about it,
Don't you agree?

You need to look beyond the walls that surround you,
To the street outside.
To all those cars going by —
One of them might one day be your ride.
That in itself is a big natural high.
So don't lose it and let it go by.
Take it slow for now and handle the ride.
You might not know where you are going,
Or what you might see,
But the world is wide open,
And that in itself is ecstasy.

I'm 49 years old.
I still feel there is so much of life left to do.
How could not you.
Deep down, you know it is true.

ADDICTIONS

Priscilla,
I don't know who you are,
Or what you are about,
But Adrian is an intense guy,
I hope you can stick it out.

He's got a great personality,
He's eager to please,
He's willing to work hard,
And, a good woman is what he needs.
Indeed.

Todd mentors him;
Because he believes in ... him... his heart... his soul.

He steers him down the right path.
Tries to teach him
No streets are paved in gold.
You have to work for your money,
Provide for your life,
And, when you can do this,
You might be blessed with a wife.

Adrian might not be there
Yet in high standing,
But if God has given him you,
He knows Adrian is mending.
Trying to be better
Than he was before.

Good luck honey, God bless you
I hope you both soar.

You will never go wrong
With God by your side.

Whatever you both do
From here on out...
Do it with pride.

He doesn't expect us to be perfect...
He knows we sometimes fail.

But...
One thing you got to remember.
You only think you can hide.
The world may believe you...
But from God – he sees your insides.
You cannot hide from our creator;
And when he sees
Your game plan
Includes him,
Only then... will you succeed.

In putting this into my book,
As an afterthought I have to conclude...
That cracker lost the girl who tried to stay true blue.
His healing was falsely on the surface
Not from within.
He wasn't ready to have love in his life.
His demons are too settled in –
He believes – she was the problem, not him.

So for right now — Crack cocaine wins.
This is a drug no one should ever begin.
And, it's just a sad reality
When people refuse to see...
Their addiction is the problem.
Not you or me.

Months later...
Priscilla finds out she is pregnant with his baby.
They are now living together in a new place,
Trying to be better for the upcoming child's sake.
Adrian has never had a child of his own,
And maybe this little one
Will help him become a man.
We can only pray
His heart will be renewed again,
When this new little heart is added to him.

The beautiful girl born in March —
Adrian tried to give away — He couldn't stand the thought
Of having to share his lot. But Priscilla didn't agree —
Left Adrian, and took her baby back home, to her family.
We are devastated that he chose to ignore God's will
And his baby. It saddens us greatly...
But we still have to pray that he will make it right one day.
This is all we can do, and this is all I can say.

ADDICTIONS

Tom —
You've been weighing on my mind — A long time now.
You finally got away from all that's been dismay.
You've changed your life so dramatically already...
Don't stop now.
You think you are taking it easy,
But you are not relaxed at all.

You're ADDICTION —
Wants the most out of life. Right here — Right now.

And, I'm here to say relax and let yourself grow up.
You are a handsome tall lean machine w/ a big heart.
But not an adult yet — You're 15.
You need to channel that huge drive,
Put it on things that you are letting pass by.
You can't keep saying you'll start next year.
So many people spent their lives saying that,
And, next year never got here.

How different would you feel right now,
If you had went out for basketball?
You love that sport a lot you know.
To get through 8 hours a day of school.
Feeling good when this part of the day is done,
Because you got ere done;
Now the rest of the day is your own.
SERIOUSLY TOM — 3 1/2 years of school left...
And then —

You don't ever have to go to school again
In your life.
Unless it's your own choice.

You'll be 18 1/2 when you graduate.
Do you understand that?
You'll still be young.
With a few more years to go until you're 21.
And, only a year and a half to go,
Before you are carrying that driver's license
In your hip pocket,
You know.
Don't worry now about getting money every day,
And seeking a bud to always come your way.
When that is your main thought per-se,
It is not enjoyable anymore.
You are driving yourself in the wrong way.

Yes, hanging out is definitely cool,
But it is more enjoyable when you don't ditch school.
Show yourself there is no reason to be a fool.
This is your job right now,
Whatever you have to do,
Can wait until after school.
You should be strict on yourself right now,
Enforcing this rule.

Do you see the line that shows you how to succeed?
Going to school.
Joining a sport.
Driver's License.

Part time job.
Your own car.
Graduating High School (you would be the 1st in the family)
This is where your drive should be.
What are you in such a hurry to grow up and do?
Because, you are going about it in the wrong ways.
You have done petty minor stuff – okay when you are young.
But the older you get – no longer are you just a pest.
The system starts looking down at you –
Now you are just a problem and a waste of their time.
They won't hesitate anymore to lock you up.
Punishment now gets harder when you are doing time.

Ask Michael – he lost most of his teenage years
Thinking he was smarter.
Thought he could skate right by.
He was so well known on his football team.
For him, people would cheer.
If his coach ever needed the football –
Mike got that ball there.

Mike was a hero and good guy in so many ways –
Then the courts pulled him out of school,
The middle of his freshman year.
Locked him up – just like that.

Instead of learning a lesson –
He started heading down the wrong path.
He was so angry at being left out and gone,
That he forgot what life was all about,
When he got out and came home.

Inside fury for what he'd missed,
And determined right away to have it all back.
His mind did not compute...
You can't ever have those missed years back.
You can only start anew.
But he refused to do that and his anger grew.
So he kept going back to jail.
Stretching 8 months or longer at a time.
He was always grateful to get out...
But then right away demanding to be given big clout.
He feels he deserves it for all the suffering he had.
He refused to work toward a goal.
He wanted it handed to him — standing right in front of him,
And when he couldn't snap his fingers fast enough
To make it happen — he went back to jail again.
Still not seeing —
The fast buck doesn't last.
For 5 years he went through this.
Did the same thing every time he got out.
Thinking he should automatically
Be standing right next to his dad.
It doesn't take years to do this dumb shit
His mind always thought and says.
His pay should equal his dads.
It wasn't handed to him and it just made him mad.

At 27, Mike's dad did get a business,
And yes, he was still young.
But he did it in all the right ways —
Working hard for many years.
Saving money, never touching it.

Stocking it away. Building up lifelong knowledge —
Opened up many a Trans. Shop for someone else,
Until he knew his time had come.

It was never simple and easy.
Scraping every penny and then some.
Now after 16 years in the business,
Yes, he can relax some;
But it is a hustle and a juggle every day.

You can take a load off when things are good —
But, you can't ever get too comfortable,
Or you're standing on pins and needles again,
Hoping work is going to come in.
So what I say is —
You have to live for the future and not just every day.
Todd always thinks ahead —
Always saves for those rainy days or months —
Because they are going to happen
Whether we like it or not.

Mike has learned to make good money the legal way...
Working for his dad,
Buying and selling cars,
Snow plowing when winter time hits hard.
The good money is more enjoyable by far.

Tom,
The reason I threw Michael into this story line mix —
I want you to learn from his mistakes.
You can avoid going through this.

It took Michael 24 years and a lot of scars.
He's doing great now,
But wishes he had done things different by far.
I want you to see — if you change it now,
No regrets when you grow up will there be.

Tom — You and Michael are both Scorpios —
Born 12 years apart on the same day.
You are both so cool, charming and I can also say...
Your Scorpion bite is one and the same.
It leads you astray.
Mike has calmed down greatly now.
Don't you wait so long to do the same.

You can get a jump start by learning now.
You learned to walk when you were young.
Start stepping down the right path — Get it done!
Don't make your life take so long to take off.
It is not necessary to always stumble and fall.
Yes, you have to stumble a little bit,
This is how we become wise after all —
But stepping into the Grand Canyon
Is not necessary at all —
Unless you happen to be out there visiting with friends,
In your own car.

Do you see honey?
You are not being damned in this world after all.
You are in the middle of growing up that's all.
You have been on this Earth only 15 years.
You have at least 60 more to go.

You are still just starting out — Don't overload yourself —
Because you're going to blow.
You are doing exactly what Michael did,
And, I'm trying to forewarn you right now —
I don't want you to lose any time out of your life.
Please don't head there — Stop — right here — right now.
You are slapping the waters in life.
Making too many waves —
Thrashing around in this No Wake Zone.
You are becoming too obvious and it won't be long,
Before you are known
In the court system.
Please don't let this be — jail is not a home.
You are going nowhere way too fast — you need to pull up —
Ease off the gas — take a step back —
If you let the dust settle — You'll find the right path.
No more waiting — next year is here!
Right now Tom — I'm begging you right here.
You should be smoothly gliding around...
Learning about life, about yourself.
Getting to know your inner thoughts and needs.
What one day you might hope to achieve.
These years right now — give you all the time you need,
To find out what it is you want to be.
That's what these growing up years are for;
They help us come into our own and shelter us
Until we are ready to brave it all alone.
Then you are almost grown — having fun;
But also working and paying your bills,
In a place of your own.
Staying on the right side of the fence,

Might sometime seem a little slow...
But it's a sure path,
No being put away for a year at a time loop hole.
So Tom — don't you see,
It is all going to come to you eventually.
Please — be a little patient.
I promise you will definitely grow up great and succeed.
I really want this for you.
But, you have to do this for you 1st,
And then do this for me ☺
I love you Tom. Endlessly.

ADDICTIONS

Ashley,
You have been on my mind, so strongly.
My mind is in a whirl wind of what I need to say,
And I pray, I do better than ok.
Your life is at stake.
I want to help balance this scale
To keep you from falling off.
Ashley, staying numb of reality is a coffin in life.
The skull & cross bones are not a happy ending.
Using a needle might seem different or cool to do,
But most of the people who thought this was cool too,
Are now deceased.
Heroine zaps the life out of you.
I know it's hard when there isn't much to do,
Small apartment,
No choice but to let the government take care of you;
Might sometimes seem like there is no way out,
But honey,
You are just starting out.
The whole world is in front of you,
And even if you can't see past the curb & driveway,
One of these days it will come together for you.
Ashley Pink, I know right now life stinks –
Looks like a dead end street,
But what you need to realize
Is that the drugs are the dead end street, not your life.
You've gotta pull through. We need you!
10 to 15 years from now,
(I know this sounds far away, but it's not)

You will be so happy that you hung in there,
And so glad you didn't let it all slip by.
Life may be doomed & bleak right now...
No job, no commited boyfriend, no car,
Maybe even no motivation,
You might not care, lack of interest,
And it's ok to feel bleak because of this —
The last years haven't been great, & it's not great right now —
You can also come out & say
You were straight when you were pregnant
And life didn't get any better...
It's your young age darling,
You haven't yet made your way in life,
So nothing is settled, and nothing is smooth.
Right now you can't see ahead, there is only dread.
When 1 in their mind sinks so low,
There only seems 1 way to go...
ASHLEY! THIS IS NOT SO!
What I see... a sweet beautiful girl
Who will find her way in the world.
She hasn't yet been very long on this earth,
But she has an understanding
Of Mother Nature's fine worth.
She started to climb the mountain and it got very steep.
She started to falter — no shoes on her feet.
It became rockier and harder, so she sat to rest.
Not realizing... she had to stay on the path.
She rested for months before she decided to climb on.
The rocky path was now betraying.
She thinks — what am I getting accomplished,
Fighting this rocky path.

For what? To be exhausted? So she again sat to rest.
Many more months go by before she starts to climb again.
The top of the mountain looks even further away.
It looks greener up there, but still rocky here.
After months of climbing, the top still looks far away...
Just too far away she thinks and says.
I don't believe I'll ever make it.
I think I'll just stay here and rest.
Ashley,
If you just stay there & rest, you will never move on.
You need to keep on climbing, you are seeing only rocks,
But if you look closer,
There are tufts of grass between those rocks,
And as you keep climbing, keep moving on,
The grass becomes stronger, the rocks smaller,
The soft moss like velvet beneath your feet.
You can't help, but to feel silly & happy & smile.
You've reached the peak!
Ashley, I know you're grown up,
But, it actually takes until we are in our 30's
Before we are really grown up,
And it's a whole different world out there, I swear!
Ashley, please keep moving on,
You haven't yet had a chance to see
All that there could be.
The drugs have put rose colored glasses on you,
And they are keeping you in a blind state of mind.
Heroine isn't living, it's the living dead,
Pills don't really help you, they eat your stomach instead.
I COMMAND THE ZOMBIE OUT OF YOU ASHLEY!
You are not alone right now, even though you feel so,

And if this is too hard to do by yourself,
Please get checked into a Center,
You need at least 6 months, and when you get out,
(Because Marseilles is a dead end zone)
Maybe you could rent a room from Mike
And get a job out here (there are lots to get)
And you know Uncle Todd & Mike
Would help you get a car.
You will be amongst lots of people,
And you will find the right boy.
Someone who wants nothing more
Than to be by your side.
Someone who loves your beautiful smile & laugh,
Your kindness and generosity, your sincerity.
Your inner and outer qualities
Make you a beautiful girl Ashley.
It's the aura that surrounds you.
The sun is shining down on this scenario,
It's a giant step and a small leap at the same time —
Ashley, you will be happy.
I swear and promise you will be just fine.
I would lay my life on the line to help save you.
This is how important you are!
I would get hit by a train, as long as I pushed you aside.
I would get shot by a gun, rather than see you bleed.
I would give up my last breath,
If it would stop you from shedding tears.
I would take the pain from 1,000 knives,
If it would again make you happy inside.
I would die for your life. That's how important you are.
Please try to reach the stars through life, not needles or pills.

I am begging you Ashley,
Please make it to the top of the mountainous hill;
Your future husband, home, children & pets
Are waiting for you,
And there are flowers to pick, family parties to plan...
I can see your decorated home, so cool man!
You'll welcome everyone w/ the smile in your eyes.
I can still see your light Ashley,
And it's waiting to be turned up high!
Destiny has a plan, and you're in it man!
Chosen people to come your way.
Life's path is waiting; let it show you the way.
The dust will settle. It will be clear as day.
I love you girl and demand harm stay out of your way.
Kick the dust onto it while you are walking
Until the harm fades away.
Endless love, hugs and kisses, from my heart to yours.
I wish upon you for the woe be gone to be cured.
Mother Nature gave us a beautiful Earth!
Let us rejoice! To your worth!
Ashley Pink, don't be blue,
Your family is here for YOU!
And...we love you.

DARKER SIDE

Written w/ sincerity
And not so regretfully

A DARKER SIDE

How sad I feel inside;
Because Mike, Shae and Chris
Are destined for this ride.
They have a mother
Who shows up 2 to 4 times a year.
She'll act like she's been there every day,
And you'd better acknowledge her dear.
Because if you don't –
You're down for the count.
She won't see you again for a long time,
Leaving you sad,
Trying to figure it out.

So act happy when she shows up
To give you 10 minutes of her time.
She will linger with you, lead you on,
And you start to think everything is fine –
But no matter how long it's been
Since she last saw you,
She'll quickly cop an attitude,
And again be through with you.
She'll start to scream –
Your life is in shambles!
You are a dirt bag!
A scum bag,
A piece of shit!
Why does she deal with you!
She goes on and on,
Working herself up to a big screaming fit.

Your towers start crumbling like pebbles,
You're sinking quick.
You hate her and love her all at the same time —
She's your mom, you need her.
Why can't she cross that line
And be happy for you, love you and say to you,
I miss you; I think you are fine.
How are you doing today, tell me what's on your mind.
This is what we pray for and cannot achieve,
But I would just like to believe — Is it so much to ask for?
I beg you on bended knees —
PLEASE OH PLEASE KAREN!
Give them what they need!
So they can move forward in life,
They need to get rid of this strife!
It all stems from you,
And deep down you know.
But you won't acknowledge it.
In your mind, they're just destined for skid row.
But no matter what —
Your demented mind has taken quite a toll,
On the ones you're supposed to love the most;
You don't want to hear it,
But I'm letting you know.
You call yourself the Queen,
And make jokes —
That everyone is a bumbling jester
Falling all over themselves to please you,
And you giggle with glee —
Your deception is hidden
So that no one will ever see —
You truly can never be pleased.

Your children are now young adults
With so much intelligence and drive.
I believe they will succeed,
And I'm also sure that when they do,
You'll show up smiling with your hand out,
Wanting to know what's in it for you.
You gave them life,
Now they'd better give back to you!

And you know what Karen,
I'm sure they will.
It's the way of the world.
Every child would always do everything
To have their mom in their life.
No matter what.
You have struck pay dirt with them.
But remember —
Nothing means anything in life
Without your family and kin.
It's the moments you are missing,
That you can't relive.

A DARKER SIDE

An evil person is buried here.
Her name is Sue,
And you'd better be scared.
She'll rear her ugly alcoholic head.
She's a darkened soul.
Better left unfed.
Don't ever unbury
What is meant to be dead;

Because she'll haunt you,
Like she haunts her family –
Storming into their house,
In the middle of the night,
Screaming drunken obscenities,
Forcing her kids out of bed.
(Two weeks ago when she was there last,
She left a pop in the fridge)
Where the hell is it!
School starts in a few hours,
But she could care less.
She is feeding on screaming,
And her screaming must be fed.
Only when the police show up,
Will she go.

Sue is still very much alive,
But everyone she meets,
Learns fast to despise
This nasty cheating evil soul,

And leaves us wondering...
Why we can't get those people
Out of our lives.
A thorn, forever stuck in the side.

A DARKER SIDE

Karen,
I have to get some animosity out of my heart.
You are such a negative in life,
That if you were a battery —
You would never start.
You are so proud to be such a bitch.
You think that makes you cool,
But it makes everyone else truly sick.
You think you are winning,
But you have only ever been sinning.
You are full of infidelity and strife,
And that's not okay
In Gods book of life.
You think you are great,
And doing okay,
Because you have friends that will pay
All those lousy bills
That comes your way.
They are just an annoyance to you,
And believe me I know —
Because after 8 years,
They are still coming to my home!
You still use my address,
Like it's yours to claim.
You haven't lived there in so long —
You are so full of shame.

There is nothing left of you
In my home or our life —

Except for your daughter,
Whom you rarely see;
You are done coming into my home
Doing as you please.

All you did was rip us off.
Taking things when you thought necessary —
Your definition of necessary... Always!

You'd hardly visit the kids
When they were around;
But if you drove by,
And saw our house sitting alone,
You'd make a beeline up our driveway,
And run into our home.
You see a roast defrosting on the counter top —
Is this what Deb's making tonight?
Then you think with delight, well —
Not any more,
Because not 1, but all 3 of my roasting pans
Just got carted out to your car;
And I know the kids told you
I make a big breakfast on Sundays.
My griddle is now gone too.

You dumb bitch —
It's your kids I am trying to feed —
Don't you get it?
I'm sure you do,
But you don't care,
Because you also take our beer,

Any clothes you think you might wear,
And feeling vindictive —
You would pull leaves off of our plants,
And break a branch or 2.

You don't ever help out —
Not one gallon of milk did we ever see;
BUT – YOU – GET – SOME – SICK – JOY
In thinking you are hurting us???
WOW.
Some more BRAIN FOOD PLEASE —
Because — this one is not registering.
And your big mouth
Always bellowing out...
Good things about yourself,
Hatred for everyone else.
You have given us nothing in return,
Except for a big headache we didn't earn.
The kids are grown up now,
And we've grown tired of you.
You are in your own world.
Maybe one day you'll join ours too.

A DARKER SIDE

We were hanging out
With our friend Ricky today.
He is a Gypsy from Romania,
And his heart has never strayed.
For many years,
He lived across the street from our shop;
Then a month ago,
They moved to a bigger house,
On a different block.

They had relatives over for dinner one night —
A mother, father, daughter and son.
Found out they have been homeless for a while now.
In Ricky and Sonia's hearts —
They knew what had to be done.
They gave their homeless relatives
Their other home, now sitting alone.
It is still mostly furnished,
And they couldn't stand the thought
Of their relatives sleeping out in the cold.

But, the relatives were not appreciative —
And within 3 to 4 weeks
Started to complain and moan...
About living in this 1 bedroom
With a carpeted basement home.

They ask Ricky and Sonia,
How could you have lived here so long in this small house?

They feel like they are being put out,
That they are getting the shady end of the deal no doubt,
Being stuck in this small house.

THE GALL! THE NERVE!
I can't believe what I have heard.

We also saw them selling some of your belongings —
They had a yard sale the other day.
We called you up Ricky and you said —
If that's what it takes
To put food on their plates, So be it.
Your kindness isn't heard.
They still don't appreciate.
They are turning into ungrateful grubby whiners
Who refuse to stand on their own 2 feet.

HOW DARE YOU — I WANT TO SAY TO THEM —
How much do you want them to bleed?
You are grownups now,
Time for you to succeed.
They can't work themselves down to the raw bones,
Just to make sure that you have a home;
And, they put you in a business too,
So that you can pay your own bills —
But your open sign is never lit up
Until it is night.
By then most people have gone home...
Are you ever going to really try?

They gave you the best —
They can give no more.
What you do from here —
It's up to you to score.

But… if you will be happier again living outdoors —
So be it; because,
Ricky and Sonia can give no more.

Lesson to be learned:
That it is a burn,
To give your heart and help somebody out,
Only to realize —
They are blood suckers — no doubt!

We won't stop giving
Because
Not everyone should be despised.

But when Leaches start sticking to your skin —
GIVE THEM A KICK IN THE ASS — SAY GOODBYE —
AND IN THE END…
Just feel good because you tried.
They were the ones who didn't want to win.

A DARKER SIDE

On my 50th birthday bash — 2010 in May,
Karen showed up to ruin my day.
She was talking of suicide.
Wanted to be begged not to die.
It was just a ploy.
How else could she show up to my party uninvited?
She starts calling people —
Talking of self-demise.
Finally got someone to say,
Come over right now.
It's okay.

She shows up at my party.
When she realized I wasn't going to throw her out —
She started drinking, laughing and carrying on.
No sign of sadness — no doubt.

Karen later comes up to me and says
We have to talk.
We went — sat in her car,
And after just a few minutes...
I wanted to punch her out!
Too much ridiculous shit coming out of her mouth.
She starts telling me of her planned demise.
She just can't be happy in life,
No matter how hard she tries.
She gets what she wants —
Does what she wants —
Goes where she wants,

And her ultimate goal —
To vacation her life away.
That's all she ever wanted to really do anyway.
Bottom line she tells me —
The world lays itself at her feet.
She has done it all,
Conquered it all,
And in the end she is still not happy.
What more is there in life for her to do?

YOU DUMB BITCH I said —
I cannot believe you were named Karen.
The only thing you can't do is care —
(About anyone other than you)
I told her — reason you can't be happy —
You lost the dream.
You gave up and walked away from the only thing in life,
That really counts —
That keeps us going —
That keeps us alive —
Our kids, our families,
And you've tossed them aside,
Like an old sock — that's too worn out —
Who cares what it was truly about?
Your only concern is yourself no doubt.

She said — my kids really love you, they tell me they do.
I said Karen, I love them too.
But the bottom line is —
They love and want their mother the most —
THAT'S YOU!
Deep down inside — They yearn for you.

She then tells me —
How proud she is of the way her son died. ???
Not many people really do it she said.
Most are like her —
They just talk the talk,
But will never take that final walk;
And, she is just so proud,
That in the end —
He actually did it,
And she praises him again.

I SAID. I SAID. I SAID.

He — was — a — little — boy.
Maybe, this is your way of acceptance,
But, I am not proud — he is now in the sky —
No longer by our side.

BREATHING SPACE

I could have given her what she asked for
Right then and there.
I wanted to choke the life out of her.
And, right then —
I wouldn't have cared.
I felt — Dared.

But, I did not touch her.

I did not want that moment to be the end of me.
Spending the rest of my life in a Penitentiary.

Instead —
I cussed and swore at her up and down.
I said —
You want a reason to live —
Then come back to your kids!
Be there for them again.
Instead of always taking, and using your mouth
To verbally tear them apart —
Try something new —
Like actually giving and feeling from your heart.
I verbally pounded this into her head.

She then tells me —
I give it to her straight, whether she likes it or not.
No one else has the guts to do that to her.
She really admires this about me;
Now, let's hug and go back to the party.
She then happily saunters away.
While for me...
Chris remained on my mind the rest of the time.

We are now nearing the end of 2010.
Karen seems to be taking a genuine interest
In the lives of her children.
I said to my stepson Mike the other day —
I feel so good that your mom is being nice to you.
I love it, I really do.
Mike said Deb — this has nothing to do with you.

But... I beg to differ. I know this is true.
No one really knows what I went through with her
On my birthday.
We were in her car for a long time that night.

So — no matter what anyone says —
If there is a starting slight change in Karen —
If it is real —
I know in part it is because of what I said.
Whatever I think of her...
I put that aside.
Her children are more important.
And —
If I could change this bitch
Even slightly for them,
I will give it a hell of a try.

And — if you don't believe me...
I gave up my 50th birthday,
For someone I sometimes don't care about.
Because — I have a heart.

Note: In the end we mellow with age,
And Karen is no exception.
She dotes on her children.
She has become a kinder person ☺
Our family is 1 again.
Amen.

A DARKER SIDE

They're all mad.
Most don't have a dad.
They are ready to kill,
Just for the thrill.
To them,
No one has ever cared.
So why should they,
They say.
The only place for them,
Is in a gang;
And this leader
They will follow
To the end.
These are our new homies man!

It's not a joke,
It's a sad mistake in life,
For the young ones growing up,
Because this leader
Won't ever let them think twice —
About how they are throwing away their life.
Do for him and you will succeed.
It is only your parents, siblings and the innocent
That is left to bleed.

Who F**king cares
When you are trying to fly high.
You'll push us to the wayside.
Don't care if we die.

This is your new family,
And through them you feel the need
To prove you can be
What you want to be.

You don't see,
That this leader is using thee.
He stands in the background,
His hands blood does not touch.
He leaves that to the patsies —
They always want to prove so much.
But they are expendable in every way.
There is always someone standing behind them,
Ready to prove their right to stay.
They don't even have to sway
These simpletons coming their way.
Seems to be,
The only time
Leaders have blood on their hands,
Is when they take out their own man,
While the gang is surrounding him.
Every gang I've ever seen,
Or watched on TV,
All think they're the baddest,
The most uncaring and mean;
But, they shoot and kill with a gun,
How simple and sad —
Or if they beat someone up,
It's 10 on 1.
I don't think they are tough and bad,
Cruel and scary is the only thought I have.

Do you know how many innocent
Children and people are dead,
And all because you look up to a guy
Who will stab you in the back.
These people
Don't even care about themselves;
They act as if they do,
But it's their anger that drives them —
They have been burned in life too.
Don't you get that?
You believe you are such a big part of something,
But the reality is,
Anger, leads to nothing.
By your own gang's initiation;
You get beat up and almost killed
Just to prove your wherewithal
Can withstand the ordeal;
And if you pass this test,
The next test is
You have to blast
An innocent person
To earn your badge,
Or graffiti a whole block of buildings,
Making them look ugly and sad.
You take from all the people,
Who try to get by in life —
The ones who work so hard to make it right.
Do you see how backwards your thinking be?
The government already takes
So much from us endlessly.
We the common person suffers from them,

Then you also make us suffer,
Again and again.

Whose side are you on?
You think it's your own,
But as you can see...
You are just the darker side of the government
I believe.
And, did you know
The town officials
Give tickets to those buildings,
Punishing them
For having graffiti on their walls.
So in essence,
You burned us,
Then help the government
Burn us some more.
You think our towns and courts deserve more money?
You don't think they get enough from us already?
Listen Dudes —
We are you, and you are us.
Stop taking from your own self.
It isn't right.
It isn't just.
Anyone can pull the trigger on a gun.
Even the smallest child.
Brains —
It takes none.
Want to prove you're smart?
Take those bullets out.
Fight 1 on 1 with your big bad fists,

Then it's not possible
For that stray bullet going through the wall
To kill the innocent.
Someone who breathes and is alive,
But someone who might not be
If you have a gun by your side.
Life is hard enough.
Why on us are you so rough?
We are all struggling too.
The things that you've been dealt in life —
¾ of this population
Was dealt the same hand too.
We have just as many problems as do you.
Don't you see?
We are all trying to succeed.
Let's end the violence please.
Stop trying to beat up on humanity.
Quit punishing the elderly, the young and the weak.
What you are doing is self-defeat.
You can still be big and bad,
But you will be looked up to even more,
When no longer
An innocent life is being had.
Be the keeper, not the reaper.
I beg of you for all mankind,
Let's together brave these tough times.
Because...
We are all in it together.
Not just one against the other.
Don't you see — ?
This is all of our America.

We've got no time for hostility.
Bigger battles are going on.
Our life's economy is hitting rock bottom.
I just want to say...
There is nothing wrong with being in a gang.
You can be who you are,
You can do your own thing,
You can be your own family,
Without terrorizing the streets.
It's okay to feel angry and mean,
But acting on it is something different entirely.
Unless you go to a garage or a gym —
Beat up that punching bag,
Get your aggression out.
Without a life being had,
Without any more being snuffed out.
As long as you are not destroying other people's lives,
Good luck, God bless.
Enjoy hanging out with the guys.

A DARKER SIDE

I am so angry right now.
I want to run into the forest and scream;
And scream and scream.
Like I have never screamed before.
Until I can't scream anymore.
Until my throat closes up,
And I fall to the bumpy floor.
Unable to breathe.
Almost until...
I can't breathe anymore.
I need to be that close
To come back around,
That's for sure.
For me,
That'd be the cure.
Except —
For all the animals that live on this land.
The forest is littered with them,
And to them...
I cannot raise my voice.
Cannot scream out to the land.
I can let nothing so ugly
Travel out to all of them.
Maybe that's why I am so big.
Distraught
Filling me up within.

My mind is racing,
There is no relief.

I'm so damn tired,
But I just can't sleep.
My stomach has grown.
My teeth are forlorn.
My smile has receded.
I'm 1 big frown.
I am not the person I used to be.
Didn't know I was leaving town.
When did I exactly leave..?
I am unsure of that moment.
Unsure of who I am right now.
I have seen better days,
And next summer is so near.
Ha ha ha. That's funny.
It's July.
Summer —
It's already here.
And I am lost inside of me somewhere.
Help is not near.
This is the biggest time
I am in fear.

Like —
I'm going down.
I'm sinking fast.
Will someone show me
How to get off this path.
On it I cannot last.
There has to be a way.
I hope I find it one day;
Before I am completely lost,

My kids so far away.
Please help me now,
I am begging you Lord
Show me the way.
I will obey —
But, I am not near ready
To be taken away.
I am still needed,
Not everyone is ok.
If you show me the light,
Tell me everyone will be alright,
Then I would leave.
Peacefully.
But...
You'll have to take me fast.
If you let me linger,
I will last.
My will is strong.
My heart steadfast.

I may be down,
My feeling forlorn,
But whilst I'm alive
The spark in me burns on.

My drive is ultimately so wild;
Even if —
Right now —
I can't show it.
Don't know it.
Can't find it.

It is instilled in me.
It will find me...
Eventually.

The mind and body
Are quite the wonderful thing
I believe.
Hmmm...
How did all this begin?
That's right;
My Thyroid problem is where it all began.
Is this all that's really ailing me man?
I'm feeling better now.
The shades are letting
Some sunlight come in.
Turns out —
My release was my pen.
Thank you Lord,
For helping me remembering.

I am back again,
And at 51,
Being worn is no longer unheard of or new;
But I'm alive man!
Most of my senses already programed.
I just lost that Thyroid brain is all.
So many people out there...
Bigger ailments than me.
Fight endlessly.
We are all in some kind of battle I believe.
So how dare I

Not be ecstatic to be alive.
You know what?
Right now my smile is a mile wide.

I can handle anything!
I'll pass the test of time.
There is nothing wrong with me.
This is life,
And, I'm just a part of humanity.

It's all in how we choose to go.
Heavy — Or — Lite.
Hmm...
Let's take a minute,
Make sure I get this right.
Simple.
How silly I see.
What I choose not to be...
Down-trodden —
Too heavy, deep, endless, slow and cold.

The Sun —
The right choice;
And by coincidence
What I choose in life.
It's closer to Heaven you know.

Being uplifted
For God,
The one sure road.
The only way to go.

So — now
When I get down,
I sit outside;
My face tilted toward the sun.
The warmth envelopes me.
I feel Gods arms around me,
And as my anger slowly leaves,
I feel a soft breeze
Caressing me.
Once again
I am happy.

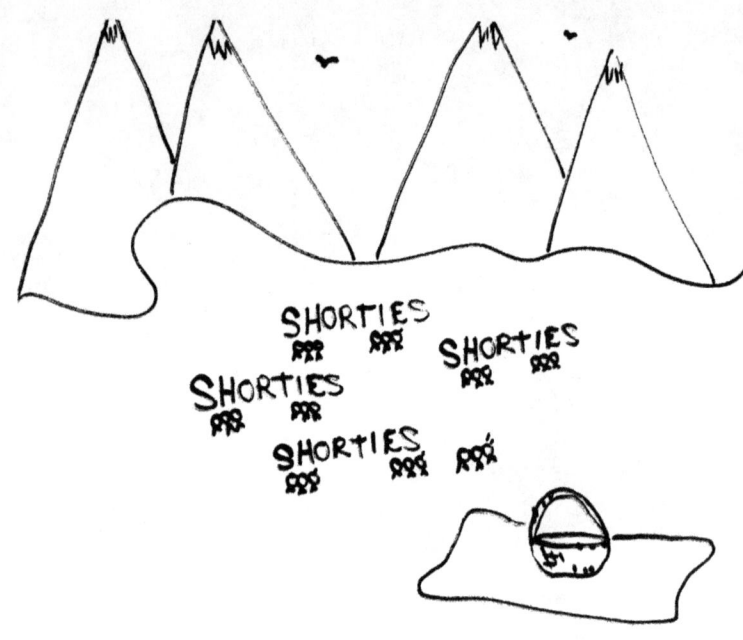

SHORTIES

Helping someone, who hurt you.
May 21st 2014
In front of the shop 1 day,
On my hands and knees,
Scrubbing shop rugs,
On the ground,
At the end of the 3rd bay.
Then...
BAM!
I was thrown forward a short distance in the air,
And, as I hit the ground,
I glanced to see what was happening;
A gold SUV backing out of the dry cleaners next store,
Not only just hit me,
Worse – didn't even realize!
Was still coming – to hit me again!
HEY! I screamed
As I summer salted / rolled out of the way.
He stopped.
Turned out to be the owner of the cleaners.
An elder Chinese man,
Who was so horrified and distraught
At what he had just done,
That I spent the next 30 minutes,
Trying to console him and reassure him.
I told him, its ok, I'm alive.
He thought we should call the ambulance and the police.
(My hands, elbows and knees were scraped & skinned)
No way! I said.

Scrapes, bumps and bruises mean nothing to me.
Seriously.
My riches in life
Will not come by destroying someone else's life.
I am okay.
He was grateful and thankful.
So was I. We hugged.
He went back to the cleaners; I walked into the shop,
And took a self-survivor picture.

"And like the sturdy ancient ruins, I am still standing" ☺

SHORTIES

Nick and Tarrah,
Tarrah and Nick,
What a beautiful baby girl.
You both were blessed.
She looks so angelic and sweet.
A great complexion,
A head full of blonde hair,
A beautiful smile,
Tiny little feet.

Enjoy her now while she is so young,
Because when she can rollover,
Your deadline has come.
She is now the boss,
And you'd better run.

This cute little stage can now touch everything.
Put it all up high,
Because she won't miss a thing —
A fuzz ball, a crumb, a hair,
It all looks good to her from down there.

Then when she crawls and walks —
Your cabinet contents come out.
It's her new hiding spot,
And she wants it cleared out.

You are in for a lot,
But I'm sure you knew

That the baby stage doesn't last long enough
For any of us.
It ends too soon.

We put her picture on the wall.
What a cute little cherub.
One day she will be bell of the ball.
Congratulations to the new mom and dad!
We love you and are proud of you
For this new little beauty that you have.

SHORTIES

We be missing you
Mikey White.
You're alright.
You're not uptight,
And pretty soon
You'll
Be back in your own
Home at night.
Feeling alright.
Only small doubts,
Left in sight —
Trying to take in,
Enough fresh air,
But that's okay,
You have the rest of your life
To do what's right,
And still live high and nice;
Because you got what it takes
To make your life great.
So — don't hesitate.
This is your fate.
Put all else behind you
Like it was a bad fall;
Because I believe
From now on,
You will be standing real tall.

SHORTIES

Ricky and Sonia,
Owen and Lola,
I hope you are having a real nice time.
Did you realize,
You left your friends behind?
Off on your journey,
Happy as can be.
A week has went into 2,
And now we are past week 3.

Your house is lit up,
But no one is inside.
Your van's not in the driveway,
And I can't remember the last time
I saw your dog outside.

I hope you are having a heck of an adventure,
And the best time ever.
Seeing relatives, a friend or 2.
Meeting new people —
HEY! Have I got a car for you!
Sell it all because you know,
When you come back the rent you will owe.

You have been gone a long time,
You are lucky it's cold;
Because your grass would now be a field,
And the wild animals would have a new home.

But don't you worry,
Have no fear —
We are the eyes and ears of your property
Right now,
And it's all still here...
Sitting vacant but dear.

I just want to ask,
One small thing if you please...
Bring back that big warm Sun.
Could you do this for me?

SHORTIES

It seems like days since I've talked to you,
And I miss you.
But —
Hey Tony,
Today the sky is bright,
Like your eyes are blue.
Todd gave me money,
And I'm sending it to you.

Guess what else is going on today?
The tow truck is coming
To haul my van away.
Out to US 30,
To be put up in the air,
Then it will be real easy,
To fix the starter from there.

There is a slight loop —
As we pushed the van into the street,
Out dark fluid leaked,
All down the driveway,
And it wasn't too sweet.
But I don't feel beat.

Like I say —
My van is going to the shop today.
Hooray!
I'll see you Thursday.
Not much else to say.

That's why I write to you in this way.
I love you son,
Have a great day.

SHORTIES

I used to have nice shapely calves,
But not today;
Because 1 has went astray.
We were out in Joliet about to cross the street.
My boyfriend grabbed my hand,
I threw my leg out to go,
Then I envisioned —
(A big rubber band that had snapped)
Was the cause of my collapse
As I fell to the street.
I couldn't move my leg at first,
Couldn't put pressure on my heel.
So, on my right tip toes,
Todd helped me limp back to the car,
Quite the ordeal.

By time we got back to the shop,
(I drove by the way)
My shoe almost wouldn't come off.
My leg was swelled so big,
About to blow,
And the bruising already prominent
From my shin to my toes.
It looked like I had frostbite,
And was about to lose my leg.
Go to the hospital now,
Everyone said.
But if you really know who I am…
I've healed myself before,
And yes I am doing it again.

As time goes on —
It is now 3 weeks.
My leg is still swollen,
And my toes are the only things
That this leg will allow
To touch the ground and meet.
I consider the hospital.
I even drive there,
But the waiting just isn't me.

So instead of getting out of my car,
I leave;
And drive home happy
That I didn't stay there
To sit endlessly.

It is now 9 weeks,
I can stand on both of my feet.
But, when the swelling went away,
I was aghast and in dismay.
My calf —
That used to be rounded out,
Now has a dimple, a dent,
Whatever you want to call it,
It's here to stay.
A mismatch has been made.
Another life's upset has just come my way.

One day at the shop,
A gentleman stopped by.
Wanted us to look at his car.

Was a doctor he said.
I seized the moment —
Told him and showed him my leg.
He said your muscle is torn,
You ripped it off the bone,
And now that muscle
Is sitting at the bottom of your leg.
How scary I said.
Is this the way it'll always be?
Yes he said.
I said — really.

So here I am,
1 nice shaped leg,
1 dimpled and worn.
I can still do all the same things,
But the appearance part is gone.
Aaa — well another thorn.
But the roses are beautiful so why be forlorn.

I really can't be,
So as they say —
Life goes on.
And, if I wasn't a smoker,
I'd still run a marathon.

SHORTIES

This shorty is the only poem in my book
That's not from me.
On Mother's Day 2010 in May,
My step son Mike wrote this for me.
I was truly pleased.

Deb,
You're a good mom,
With sons named Tony and Tom.
Monday through Friday you get out of bed,
Drive me and my dad to work
In the big red sled.
You're here for us day and night,
Especially my dad with a rub so tight.
Deb, we hope your Mother's Day is swell,
But we also hope the Hawks do well.

Later on adding this in...
Man o man!
The Blackhawks DID
Win the cup in 2010
Congrats to all of us,
And to all of them!
They did it!
The champions!

SHORTIES

Sonia,
You didn't think you could again.
It wasn't in your plan.
But now...
You're pregnant w/ your babe.
You never thought it would end.
Then all of a sudden it's over,
And the baby is in your arms.

A beautiful Boo Boo,
A little him.
A head full of dark hair.
The joy of a new beginning.
Born at the end of May,
What a beautiful day.
He's perfect in every way;
And quite the feisty guy I'd say.

He looks so little at 7 lbs.
But he's a healthy eater,
Always wants those bottles around.
He can already hold his head up,
At barely 1 week old,
This boy is soon to be everywhere,
Don't you know?

Congratulations
Ricky, Sonia, Owen and Lola.
I wish for everlasting happiness

In your household —
I'd wish for peace and quiet too,
But I don't think you are going to get that,
Do you?

Never a dull moment,
That's true;
But some commotion in your lives
Is well worth the effort.

I'm so happy for all of you guys,
That you were given this blessing
From the heavenly skies.

God smiled down on you today.
He has enriched your lives
W/ this gift from paradise.

A new beginning opened wide;
Like a rainbow that stretches from end to end.
This little pot of gold
Now rests in your hands.
You've been given the opportunity of a life time man!

Congratulations again,
How happy for you that I am.
And if you want to remain happy yourselves —
Keep those bottles on hand.
For this new little man.
So sleeping at night
Will happen again.

Of course —
Only until he crawls, walks and stands;
And, I know you are not ready to hear that yet —
So I'll finish this poem.
The end.

SHORTIES

Kelly,
A flowing flower child
You seem to me.
Spreading good will,
Like a butterfly that is free.
It's Grateful Dead till your dying days.
You are wild, passionate and crazy in some ways.
A little lost and misconstrued,
You know it is the pills
That does this to you.
Playing games with your brain,
Your mind can't live life sane.

The best part of you I know –
Happened almost 3 years ago.
You and Todd's brother Dan came,
Stayed a week.

Right away Dan took control.
His own raw heart bleeding stayed on top of the situation;
The mentor for our souls, he carried us so;
While Todd and I lay holding each other;
Feeling decrepit, lost and old.
Were we still alive? We didn't feel so.

Our hearts were fried,
Our faces lost.
We couldn't do anything,
We were just 2 piles of mush.

You and Dan moved us around.
You made sure our eating wasn't lost.
Like an angel with wings,
You took care of us,
And tended to everything.
You ran to the store.
You cleaned my house.
The Pastor,
The flowers,
Jerry Garcia's blanket.
Candles,
Angels,
And all the things
That we gathered around
While we sat outside
Feeling forlorn.

You lit that corner up,
And we all wanted to stay
Sitting right there,
Because Christopher seemed close —
We couldn't touch him,
But we could feel him there.

The very last pit stop.
It was hard to stay away from that spot.
We were drawn to it —
Even if we could change it not.

I want you to know how grateful I am,
And how much you really helped out.

While your own heart was flattened and raw,
You still big time
Helped us out by far.
You did everything we couldn't do,
You were our beacon of light.
God bless you Kelly,
And thank you.

I've thanked everyone, and I would thank everyone again.
Some people might be shocked that I'm praising Kelly.
It doesn't matter who people are in life,
When they come through and really help you...
They deserve praise too.

(I found out a year after Chris passed,
That Kelly had never gotten our card, our appreciation.
That's how this poem began.)

SHORTIES

My eyes are closed to life.
They shall not be opened anymore.
For I am sick of the heartache and pain
Life has brought.
Life has done me no justice,
But tortured me good.
I've been convicted for being born into this very world!
When will it all end?
Not now,
Not ever.
The only solution is to end it myself.
To be rid of the loneliness
And all the pain.
To kill myself is the only way.

The thoughts of some people today.
I beg of you to let me sway.
Life Can and will never be perfect — No Way.
But ultimately — Life will be okay.
It always works itself out in this way —
You just got to hang in there.
You just got to believe.
You can be saved.
The Lord will watch over Thee.
And... In your mind if you can't do it for you,
Please do it for everyone around you.

You are not alone even if you are feeling so.
1 person never gets taken out.
You leave also swallowing everyone else's heart.
There is a world of love out here for you.
This I want you to know.
Please believe me — for this is so.
I beg of you — Take it one day at a time
For every day is new; and every day you'll be 1 step closer
To understanding you.

SHORTIES

Chris and Michelle,
You got married,
And have your own house.
The best wishes I want to send —
Are big,
Not small like a mouse.

I'm glad you both found each other
In this crazy world we share;
And remember —
For each other always be there.
Nothing is more important now,
Than the life that you 2 have.

It is easy to be happy,
When life is going great,
But you need each other all the more,
When things aren't 1st rate.

No matter what we ask for,
Or what we want to prove —
It is always each other,
You 1st have to turn to.

Always strive to do better
Than your Elders did,
And you will never fall short —
Because the wisest ones teach us,
To work hard,
And follow your heart.

I love you Chris,
And I don't know you Michelle,
But if Chris has chosen you,
Then I love you as well.
Here's to a good life,
And a great start.
May your happiness
Always Top The Charts!

SHORTIES

I got my 1ˢᵗ motorized bike today.
Looks like it's from the 70's
I'd have to say.
But, I thought the 70's were great.
So I'm okay.

My boyfriend thought it was too small for him.
To me,
It looked just right.
I can see me —
Jumping and grooving,
Holding the handle bars tight.
I can't wait to feel flight.
It will suit me just right.

I rode a dirt bike,
Until I was 13.
It seemed like nothing
To jump on it,
Take off
And get mean.

Well...
I took this bike out,
For the first time the other day;
And at 51,
I'm feeling a little uneasy
I'd have to say.

A stick shift car,
No big deal;
But getting used
To this dirt bikes
Stick shift —

Well, I almost popped a wheelie
The first time I took off.
It left me feeling a little queasy —
I was almost scared to go around the block.

It's too big for me I thought.
Glad to be back in front of the shop,
I hopped right off.

Todd looked at me and said,
You have a license,
Don't you want to go around the block again?
No I said.
I'm done with that.
Maybe some other time
When I am padded up and in a field.

He smiled and said,
You're getting old,
Its okay,
It's not a big deal.

I am not getting old I said,
I just don't have the hang of it yet.

I may be long legged,
But I believe,
This bike is too big for me by far.

You poor baby he said,
Do you want to go to the tricycle store?

You're just so funny.
I swear.

You got me.
I was scared.

Then I smiled and said,
So there.

STATE APPEAL

STATE APPEAL

I'm at DCFS — Oh what a mess.
I am in need of a medical card.
I feel I'm being put through a test.
Babies are crying, people are talking.
Cell phones are ringing, people are bitching.
Names being called over the intercom,
But I can't hear a thing.
Did they call my name; did I miss the call?
I have been here for a long while.
They are starting to close the doors.

This is the ghettos place I heard someone say.
She starts bitching —
They'd better put some food into her baby's mouth today.
She don't have time for none of this shit,
Just give her link card and get her out quick,
Or she will raise hell and throw a big screaming fit!

Sit down! I finally screamed in her face.
No one told you to have 6 kids,
You are the disgrace living off the state.

Don't bitch at them because you are out of milk —
Trade in your $600 dollar cell phone
And pay some of your bills.
Do your own nails instead of getting them done —
Quit buying designer clothes
While your children have hand me downs.

Why don't you care?
Instead of feeling like everyone else should —
In the land of opportunity any job is good.

Start taking care of your own kids,
Quit making the world pay,
For you waiting to get the link card
Just to trade for some cash today.
It is not our place to make sure your lavish lifestyle stays.
Our only investment —
Is the promise that babies grow up healthy today.
It is not to give oodles of coddles
To the moms that had the babes,
So get off your high horse bitch,
You've already got it made.

I am in need of a medical card.
My ailments won't go away.
So no one here is feeling sorry for you today.
Did you hear me? Sit down I say!

Then a lady walks out and says,
Who has been here since before 4?
I have I shout — I jump out of my seat,
She takes me to her desk but nothing is neat.
It seems —
I was never processed 3 months ago the day I first came.
Now I am starting all over again to wait and see,
What didn't come before — will it come this time?
No one knows for sure.
A hit or a miss.
You go through a lot to score.

I probably sound as bad as the girl who bitched,
But my medical attention requires more
Than I have money for.

Hundreds of dollars
For less than an hour of doctors' time,
And if you are a hard worker with no insurance,
There are no breaks of any kind.

We are pushed into this circumstance
By our society today.
Cash doesn't give you a break anymore.
All I can do is go home and pray —
That this new lady will do what she is supposed to do.
Put my information through.

My medical card is now 4 months overdue.
Thank God I am a fighter,
Otherwise I'd be through.

They are damning the honest and true.

They feed into the whiney,
While the rest struggle to live like the poor.
What a sad score.
Our hard work means nothing more.

STATE APPEAL

I was watching the news on TV today.
Hearing discerning words come my way.
They talk of the terrible things
Leading people to be overweight.
They accuse snack machines,
Ice cream machines and food vendors
Of being a big culprit and cause,
And restaurants they dam,
For the meat and potatoes always plentiful and on hand.
They think vending machines should be tossed.
The meat and potatoes should be lost.
Are they serious?
Did I hear this correctly?
To cut out another big chunk of our society —
What about all those working vendors and their families?
The restaurants and their employees?
This is our free society?
I believe it's being hacked at and taken away.
Why are we the ones who always have to pay?

We the people are in a constant state of recession —
But all the higher ups have their own jets.
They couldn't possibly fly 1st class.
The President, the Pope and the Armed Forces
Are the only ones who should be honored with that.
As for the rest of them,
Why should we have to pay,
So from us they could stay away?

The Governments are here
To keep peace and ensure equality;
But they are not in dismay,
They just keep all of us this way.
Does this make sense?
We were shown the horrors of Hitler
From the time we were kids,
And told his government is so bad
That we are lucky it is America we have.
Yet more and more we have no say,
And more and more they continue to take away.
I am a Republican in the State of Illinois,
But —
Illinois is a Democratic State —
So what does my vote mean?
It doesn't mean anything.

We are a society stuck between 2 pieces of glass.
We are all just ants.
Trying to make our home and our way,
But the big-wigs
Are holding our world between their hands
And shaking it up and down like an Etch a Sketch —
Telling us...
Devastation has come to our land!
We now have to pay even more
To fix the problem at hand.
And this is our land?
That is a joke by sleight of hand.
They are all magicians,
And even if we see the blunder it matters not.

What is the land of the free?
Because we are being taxed
Out of our businesses and homes quickly.

Just so you know,
I am not anti-government or antiwar.
I am just a human being
Trying to keep my head above water,
At the very least get by,
And not be chastised in the meantime for being alive.

Science also spends unheard of amounts of money
Trying to clone these days.
The world is already overpopulated now I'd say.
Do we really need to make
More animals and people in artificial ways?
Maybe these are the type of jobs we should cut out.
Billions of dollars to see and create what we already know —
Procreation began with Adam and Eve so very long ago,
And since the beginning of time...
We, and the animals
Have already learned how to make our own kind.
Now we strive —
Give up almost everything fun and nice,
To pay for the world —
So they could live right?
What about us and our plight?
We are just as deserving,
Isn't this right?
What would,
The Town,

City,
State,
And Country Governments be,
If there was no population ...
Just them — And not you or me?

We are very important you see.
The Governments need us as much as we need them,
And we — Not just them deserve a better leg to stand on.
Because...
They are living large and raking in the dough,
While we are trying to stop ourselves from sinking.
You know?

These hard times are for whom?
Oh! That's right!
Not them...Us again.
We are the ones who get damned
And it makes me angry as hell —
Because the Governments never have to worry or dwell,
On making it through everyday life.

That is left for us...
Dress warm —
Try not to get sick —
Stretch that dollar —
We have proven it is possible on a family of 6.
We'll get you in this house for a real good price,
And, if you do believe it —
6 months later...
It's being taken away,

Because you're Mortgage just tripled in size,
And with your pay that doesn't coincide.

Way to beat down
The people that thought they were still standing.
I wonder how many more properties are in foreclosure now.

Used to be...
If you put a fence around your property it was yours.
Now your little plot of land can never be paid off.
In whose hair brained idea did this occur?
How can the Governments ensure that it is all theirs?
Where is Gods signing off signature?
How did the Governments get the lien?
What did they pay to acquire the Earth and all its lands,
That they could so off handedly
Make everyone forever pay out of pocket and hand,
And raise it on command,
By just sitting in a board room with a show of hands?

I understand we all have to do our part,
But is it really fair to squeeze from us every last drop,
And then have the nerve to say —
The Deficit grows larger,
And the average family?
Sorry.
You are the ones who have to pay.

And what about the Elderly today?
Is it necessary to take from them until they die?
In old times —

The Elderly were considered sacred.
Now if we live to a ripe old age,
High five the Governments say.

You don't want us to drink.
You don't want us to smoke.
You don't want us to buy convenient on the go snacks.
You don't want us to order out
From a fast food restaurant.
When most people have 2 jobs in these times,
Why must you still tighten the lines?

If only 1 person in the family needed to work these days;
Most everyone who needed a job would already have one,
And not be in dismay.

And, what about the taxes that is due 2 times a year?
I feel we're tricked into paying 55% up front,
And the lessor amount due at years end?
Ends up costing us more than it did in the beginning.

Less than a month before 2010's December tax was due —
They incredulously raised it,
And wouldn't wait the three months
Until after the year was new,
To put it into the next tax bill.

I also heard the TV say —
If the people want good medical
Then the people have to pay!

We shouldn't have to lose our homes, or our lives
Over a medical bill.
NO Way!
I believe —
In the taxes that we endlessly ever faithfully do pay,
Should already have included medical.
This is the right way.
Where for art thou in our time of suffering
Plain and loud?
The people in the world are begging you PLEASE!
Think of us!
Obviously we are here for you!
Can we ever get a glimpse of sunny days coming through?

You are forcing us to build a Pyramid
Without directly saying so.
How dare you be so bold!
We are also what life is all about!

Who say you should be given all the clout?
Let's ante it up and even it out.
This is America right?
This time I stand out loud.

We don't deserve to be shackled in an invisible hold.
God has our souls and not the Governments,
Truth be told.
It is our pocket books that they hold,
And we are seemingly left feeling cold.

Slowly damning our lives.
2012 is looking right.
The beginning of the end by man's sleight of hand.
Thou art thought ye to be too powerful —
A grave mistake.
We will slowly die this human race.
All the power and money in the world
Cannot replace the end if us.
Do you see what is at stake?
I beseech to this world —
Give back to our human race before it is too late,
Because in the end…
You guys have the upper hand.
I beg you to make amends!
Would you truly let us end?
Feel in your hearts the sun again,
And the laughter that is still in the land.
Come on man!
You can do it!
I know you can.
Isn't the United States supposed to be for the people?
Or is that now considered old school and bland.
Because we're not feeling it anymore.
Do you understand —

STATE APPEAL

I went to see the town Mayor the other day.
His office was dark and empty.
He's rarely there they say.
(They) being the secretaries and staff.
They are here every day,
While the Mayor's office sits vacant and dark.
Like the Emperor's new clothes,
The naked eye sees him not.
At the once a month town meeting
You can view him in his seat.
You are even allowed to speak.
But don't say too much.
They'll shut you up, sit you down.
They don't want to change anything,
And are bored with our version of what is wrong.
We are the ones that house them, put shoes on their feet –
That gives them their seat;
But somehow they forget this
In their fattened pockets of deceit.
And the town official
Who really wants to make a difference?
I know an upstanding guy named Joe.
He is someone who is for his community.
Wants to see it grow, not eventually fold.
Well he voted against the panel one day.
He couldn't see spending $30,000 on a fire work display,
That within an hour is done;
Especially when last year was a bust.
The rain wouldn't stop coming;

And when they finally decided to set them off...
Not many of the town folk showed up.
Joe explains where this money needs to go.
He sees all the streets that are in decay.
The vicious pot holes growing larger in every way.
Seeing more homeless every day.
People moving out of their homes
Because they can no longer afford to pay
The outrageous taxes that outmatch their pay.
Let's spend the money the right way.
Give back to the town Joe says.
Silence greeted his request.
He was voted down.

What the selfish panel wants is in,
And a real person like Joe
Who was later running for Mayor and about to win
Was pushed to the way side.
Somehow —
Extra votes appeared.
Where did these people come from?
How were they able to vote?
Were they licensed and registered?
Whatever happened was under handed for sure.
It's like only the selfish and greedy can be put into power.
People who don't really care
About this town, or this Earth.
This is what the city does
When a Dudley Do Right like Joe
Fights for the cause.
They run this town!

Therefore the money stay's greasing their palms.
Joe may have won the preliminary,
But on voting day he was stopped in his tracks.
It's their land he's stepping on and they won't have it.
Just so everyone knows it is a fact.
Joe lost the election.
Just like that.
How sad.
In running for Mayor, Joe had to give up his seat.
Now he's ousted completely.
The greasy palms stay greased.
I even heard our President Laugh and say —
They want the average family to keep suffering,
While people in power like him keep getting a raise.
Can you believe this he says?
I don't think this is one bit funny.
These light hearted snickers seem to laugh in our face,
Boldly letting us know we are being put in our place.
The gavel endlessly pounding against the human race.
Is it fair — no its not.
Can we do anything about it?
The government says they'll look into it.
We now have photo enforced lights.
No police involved.
And at $100 a picture they are laughing out loud.
They can now punish us by video
While they sit fat in their seat.
Click-Click-Click
It's all handled for them — how sweet.
Is this what is taking tops?
Revenue for cities and towns.

Buildings broken into, graffiti,
And where are the cops driving around?
In the parking lots of our stores and restaurants
Running tags, looking for someone to tow
Or lay a ticket on —
The big hit of the day!
The average person is now more criminal
Than stealing, destruction,
And life threatening I'd say.
Hell — you could stay home for the day.
They'll walk right in your yard,
And ticket your car in the driveway.
And speaking of property...
I heard taxes are on the rise again.
Come on man! Who are they kidding!
Didn't they just do that at the end of 2010?
Is this the big ball they're waiting to drop?
While businesses are shutting down and
Houses are abandoned, closed up.
So many need a job and a home...
But the cities and towns
Arn't willing to lower anything down.
It's like our graves are pre dug,
And they are shoveling the dirt in
Faster than we can dig it out.
Their endless truck loads overwhelm us,
And the tiny spoons they give us to work with
Hold no clout —
Shovels have been banned.
They're considered dangerous now.
Making sure we never get far.

Yet, they still demand more.
It's hard to believe they are gunning for a ghost town,
But the dominos are in motion
And the signs are all around.
A reprieve is what we need.
We hope the right way will be found.
This is what we hope for.
What keeps us moving on.
Like steadfast tin soldiers,
Always honorable we are duty bound;
And...
We'll remain this way till the sun does shine no more.
That will be the day when we realize there is no cure.
Until then, we'll blindly keep our hopes up.
That's for sure.
What I would like to say in the end
To Joe, who is a good man —
Thank you for trying my friend, your cause was worthy,
And I commend you for taking a stand.
Wish they all had a heart like yours. We'd be happy again.

STATE APPEAL

I am so appalled,
I want to scream out loud.
I bought a '94 Lexus
For $300 bucks.
It needed an engine.
That's what sucks.
It took a couple of months
To get the one I need,
And when this car was running,
I drove straight to the Driver Facility.
(99th & King Drive)
They handle it all there.
I get it plated,
Put in my name,
And pay the taxes the State so claims.
This was in April 2012.
I did what I was supposed to.
All is well.
Now it is the end of December,
4 days before the New Year's bell tolls.
I get a letter in the mail,
Stating taxes I owe
On my '94 Lexus,
From almost a year ago.
I tossed the paper away,
Thinking it's a scam or joke,
And went about my day
In my normal pleasant way.
Later in my car

I get stopped at a light.
My thoughts start bugging me...
I reach into my glove box and see,
My car papers are showing
I have paid the taxes indeed.
I start to feel angry.
When I got home,
I pulled that paper
Out of the trash
And called this facility —
Demanding — how dare they send this paper to me.
I paid my taxes,
The proof is right in front of me.
She basically said to me,
The taxes you paid on that paper don't count.
You paid to the State,
And earlier this year
Cook County came out
Decided from now on,
With every car bought
They also deserved a cut???
This is what your paper is all about,
Which means your taxes were not paid,
And the amount shown must be paid in full.
You have 30 days.
I said...
What is going on here?
Are they nuts?
I was never informed
The day I plated my car —
I found out...

It is not the place of the State facility
To inform us of this new greed.
I am shocked — speechless.
I just can't believe...
Not only
Did they throw this on me,
Also the fact,
Cook County wants 7x the amount
That the State took from me.
Seriously?
For my '94 Lexus w/ 200.000 + miles.
I am now paying more to be legal
Than what this car is worth,
And the bottom crushing line is
I haven't worked in a while.
I am told it's not their problem,
It's mine.
Now I see the dividing line.
The Governments against the rest of mankind.
How did this all change over time???
Growing up in school,
We learned about Leaders,
People in power.
Some of them we were taught to despise.
Now you are the ones
Trying to cook us alive.
Is this what our Nation should be compared to???
Our governments were formed
To take care of us.
That all is even.
Let there be trust.

Yet,
Everything we believed in
Is being pushed to the side.
We're treated like animals.
This fact you don't anymore hide.
People get jailed for treating their pets this way,
But the governments suffer no repercussions.
No punishment is made.
Do you think if us people honestly had a vote in life
This would be our chosen way?
That we would so willingly throw our lives away?
Like slaves back in the Egyptian days?
Families split up — Everyone has to work.
Suffering — endlessly,
While the Rulers
Bask in riches and glory.
The thinning of the herd
Is the era of our day.
How proud you must be
Of this new escapade.
It sickens me greatly.
This falsehood from which you were made.
You are no longer here for us.
Your heart now,
Only warms you're your own way.
What dismay for us people today.

Summation:

Do you realize in the simplicity of what I am saying?

From the time I was small,

Besides vitamin D milk, I was raised on Pepsi.

I grew up athletic, lean, and tall.

It's not the sugary pop.

It's not the fast food.

It's not the absent parent.

It's the government.

When times were right,

The men worked.

The women stayed home.

She kept the kids, the house, made the dinner.

The men come in at sundown, their work day done.

The kids were not unruly.

They appreciated their family, their home, their life.

Now governments take this away.

Taxing over the top of the line

Is why we're where we are today.

Fake substitutes — You say its better this way.

Both parents have to work.

The kids are left alone.

We are running to fast food restaurants.

It's too late to cook dinner when we get home.

Prices are too high.

Income is too low.

You are taxing the hell OUT of us,

Yet, hell is what we know.

It's what you show.

Forcing this suffering upon us.

Young, middle-aged, old.

Stripped, taxed, cold.
Taxed, taxed, taxed.
This same dollar.
Again. Again. Again.
I think you the governments
Is the hoarders' man,
While we the people remain condemned.
Can you throw away this life sentence?
Where's the one with heart?
With helping hands?
Is going to heaven after we've passed
The only way to be welcomed home again?

I hit the nail on the head.
How sad.
Aren't you sorry man?
I am.

BAD HABITS

BAD HABITS

My bad habit is easy to see.
I am a cigarette smoker,
And full flavor menthols,
Is what I choose indeed.

I enjoy them too much,
To take only small puffs.
How hard do I hit?
I smoke them up quick.
I don't like to waste them,
Not one little bit.

My boyfriend goes crazy around me,
Because...
He can't stand to see
Our front room
Fill up with smoke;
But I never notice that.
It's no joke.

I don't get what he says,
Because he is a smoker too.
Although a pack will last him 4 days,
And in 1 day my pack is through.
But he is a non-menthol smoker you see,
So I can understand his longevity.

His cigarettes are dry,
Give me a headache,

Bother my throat;
But my menthols are refreshing,
They get me stoked.

Todd hates the smell.
I know that all too well,
Because he will yell...
Would you put that thing out!
For Christ sake it smells!
You are smoking the filter!

But...I know damn well —
The tobacco goes past the white into the brown.
So if the white is still showing,
I can't put it down.

There are still a couple of hits
Left on that cigarette.
I am not ready
To put it out just yet.
And after 10 years,
Todd has put up with me quite well.
Although I have to say,
He still grumbles about it to this day.

But...I am a smoker,
So what can I say —?

Except...
With my cigarettes in hand,
A bottle of Pepsi,

Or Budweiser beer —
I am ready to cheer!
For the Black Hawks! The White Sox! The Chicago Bears!
I try to love the Cubbies,
But my heart just isn't there.

I watch them mostly at home,
Because I can't smoke out there,
Which doesn't seem fair
When you are sitting outside.
My cigarette smoke means nothing,
When all the Industrial is close by...
Clouding our vision from the sky,
Smoking 24 hours a day,
And at least I can say,
When I am sleeping,
My smoking is nay.

And to all the big wigs who say,
In buildings we can no longer smoke,
Are the ones whose paycheck is getting fatter,
By the cigarette taxes that they invoke.

If we raise the taxes they say,
The smokers will slow down,
They won't want to pay.

What bullshit I say!
Because they know smokers are here to stay.

So —
They happily raise the tax,
Again and again.
Fattening their pockets,
While we are called the smokers from hell.
Is there no end?

They chastise us,
And want us to hide away;
But they are happily taking our tax money,
And stocking it away.
Off to the bank they go...
And —
I'll bet those tires are smoking all the way!
More so than the cigarette I am enjoying right now I'd say.

But —
My opinion I don't shout.
I just write it down in thought.
Because it does no good to complain,
When there are so many,
And not just one to blame.

So I'll relax,
And smoke my cigarette
In the land of the free.
You can have all my tax dollars,
But you won't stop me.
Because...
I am still smoking
In your public facilities.

BAD HABITS

I sacrificed my love of beer
For lent this year.
The going has been rough.
I'm freaking out.
Yet I remain tough.
I have complained,
And people have complained at me
When I complain;
But, I think...
Complaining is a good thing.
If it didn't bother me,
It wouldn't be a sacrifice.
Isn't this right?
I wouldn't have given anything up.
I would have only lied.
But —
This is not what's happening here.
Because —
I love my beer.
A relaxing beer
At the end of the day.
A beer while cooking dinner sometimes
Is the way.
Sitting outside w/ a beer in my hand.
Swinging back and forth,
While friends throw horseshoes
Across the yard.
Our neighbors sitting on their porch,
We chat from afar.

Doing yard work.
Busting ass.
A beer taste so good,
It goes down fast!
A beer when I'm happy.
A beer when I'm not.
A beer to cheer,
Love, life, friends
And family so dear.
BUT...
You know now what I am noticing here?
I am sitting here straight,
While everyone is drinking beer.
They are so loud,
It's hurting my head.
They're jamming, jumping, yelling,
Playing pool until 2am.
All I want is to go home to bed.
I'm hearing the same conversations,
Over and over again.
The same subject,
They don't remember they just said.
I am now the designated driver.
No one is willing to wrap this up.
Full throttle they push on.
I will only get home,
When the beer is out.
I try to hide some.
I get found out.
They cheer some more.
A toast to me,

Because I am not drinking beer.
They think this will appease me.
They are taking advantage of me.
What a nightmare!

In these 46 days my testing is clear.
Our transmission rebuilder had a stroke
The very next day.
From then on...
It was kayos!
Kayos that wasn't going to go away.
Our friend Jeff is a builder.
He promised to come in every night
After his work day was done.
Todd's son Michael also came in to help him out.
We all pulled together.
We had to get these cars out.
Larry, our builder is alive,
But in a bad way.
He has no movement
On 1 side.
Lengthy therapy is the only way.
3 months they say.

We paid Larry's rent for the upcoming month.
We helped his son out.
This was a must.
Inside, I was going nuts!
I've had people tell me to drink a mixed drink,
Seeing as I only gave up beer,
And... those weekends don't count;

Monday through Friday
Is what lent's all about.
This doesn't sound right.
I go to the internet, which says,
To indulge on weekends
Is considered okay.
Not in my mind.
No alcohol! No way!
We were now at the shop
For so many hours,
I felt I was never home.
What do you do when you work all day,
Then stay at work ½ the night?
You have a beer,
Because your designated driver is sitting right here!
Every night seemed the same.
Getting home between 10pm to 2am,
Still not finished with my day.
I made dinner most every night —
It mattered not the time;
Threw a load in the wash,
Staying positive in my thoughts;
Thinking... by time this is done,
I'll have some weight loss.

On the final day at midnight,
Lent comes to an end.
I can't wait to have a beer.
I get one, but I leave it sitting there.
It took me a while to have the 1st drink.
I felt beer shy this 1st couple of weeks.

In the end...
I proudly did the whole 46 days.
I am humbled in Gods praise.
I am humbled from within, for him.
Amen.

THE EYES HAVE IT

THE EYES HAVE IT

I have bright blue eyes,
Not a big deal to me.
This color runs all through my family.
Different brightness, tones and hues,
But still the same in my book of blues.

Strangers react surprised when they see my eyes.
They can't believe how blue they are.
Some of them act mesmerized.
That's a joke,
They're just being silly.
There are lots of beautiful eyes out there,
Sparkling brown eyes,
Are the ones that make me stop and stare.

My sister is a little different,
Her eyes are hazel, sometimes blue;
But, they can also look very green,
And they are beautiful when they create their own hue.

My son when he was born,
Had the most beautiful eyes that anyone could adorn.
A shockingly deep violet blue,
A sight to be seen I tell you true.
A color to me never before shown
In the eyes of a human being,
But now it is known – or –
At least I have the pictures to prove this is so,
Because when he turned 3,

His eyes changed color, overnight, instantly.
They are now light blue,
And in sync with the rest of my family.

My boyfriend loves the knowledge game show on TV.
He thinks the announcer is the best.
I think his eyes are as dark as a shark.
When we watch the show, I always stare at his eyes.
They are amazing to me, dark and mysterious,
The kind that take command;
But I hear he is actually a very nice man.

Then there is a different kind of eyes.
Where color doesn't matter.
They are the sad eyes, the despondent eyes,
The eyes that have given up hope.
The life gone out of the eyes, the eyes of hunger —
These are the saddest eyes to look at,
The ones that hurt the most.
We feel instant compassion — They tug at our heart.
But we can't change what we see in passing,
Our limited life style has spoke.

Then there are the ugly eyes, the angry eyes,
The eyes that look dead.
They have no compassion, no soul.
These are the eyes to be scared of.
These eyes will leave you cold;
And in an overcrowded room, you'll feel quite alone.
Be wary when these eyes are around,
Because —

They could zap the life out of you,
Without even making a sound.

Then there are the smiling eyes, the laughing eyes,
The eyes that light up a room.
You can't help but to feel good when you see these eyes,
It can never be too soon.
These are the eyes that make the world bloom.

Then there are the eyes that don't get to see.
Their perception is way different than you or me.
They can't use their eyes,
But their other senses are magnified.
We can only hope one day that all eyes will get to see.
With all of our current scientific knowledge,
I believe this should be a strong possibility.

Then there are the eyes of wisdom,
And the eyes of knowledge.
They have already lived a lifetime or so.
Way beyond our years —
These eyes hold everything in them very dear.
To the edge of the world and back —
These eyes are quite packed.

There are so many styles of eyes,
Similar in shape and size.
But each one individual.
Like DNA, we are all unique in our own way.

Angels on Earth

ANGELS ON EARTH

Mom,
I want to tell you from my heart,
How much you mean to me
In my life throughout.
I was rebellious.
Free spirited.
Determined to run around on my own —
But YOU made the place that I called home.
Before you moved to Tennessee,
The holidays at your house,
Were the most special.
Indeed.
I never felt a holiday was near,
Until I'd go to your house
And find…
The holidays were alive in here!
My spirit would lift up,
My being on the rise,
Just being around you
Put the sun in my skies,
The lift in my step,
The smile in my eyes.
Mom,
I do not want to wait
Until you die
To say how much I love you —
To tell you how I feel inside.
I wasn't the best child.
I took more than I gave.

Still,
You were always here for me.
You never strayed.
Mom,
You are my tree of life.
Throughout all my years,
Your lovely branches,
Have sprouted beautiful flowers…
Teaching me.
Sheltering me.
Helping me grow.
My love for animals.
Perseverance.
Right from wrong.
I have made it so far in life,
Mostly because of you —
You are why I always smile ☺
Did you know?
This is true.
You've put aside all your needs,
To make sure
We kids grew up nicely.
I am indebted in your generosity.
I want you to know,
How special you are —
How special you will always be.
I wish I could win the lottery,
And give back to you.
For Eternity.
To see you living comfortably
For the rest of your life…

Would be my dream come true.
I wish this on a star.
Every night for you.
Alas,
I only have my words in writing.
My heart is pounding.
This heart that you give to me.
So freely.
I cherish you dearly.
You mean the world to me.
I love you mommy.

ANGELS ON EARTH

Karen,
From the day I first met you I could see,
Your kindness, your sincerity,
Your genuine apathy.
Your worldly knowledge that surpassed me,
You used it to kindly teach me.
I felt you were in tune with me,
And, you saw things I couldn't see;
But, I also saw a lot in you.
Karen, you got divorced when your boys were so young.
Forced to take complete control of your lives,
Now both a father and a mom.
You were devastated and hurt,
But that didn't stop you from moving on.
Hard to take time feeling sorry for yourself.
Your kids came 1st.
3 of them solely depending on their mom.
Then you met Mr. Bill,
And you could finally see,
The light at the end of the tunnel.
The light coming from he.
How blessed and happy.
Bill has 2 daughters of his own.
2 of your boys have dark hair,
His girls and your other son blonde.
The perfect family.
Not only a dad to go along with the mom,
But someone who truly loves you.
Your life partner was found.

Happiness had finally come.
You're struggling for many years,
Can now relax some.
Karen, you are beautiful, almost perfect.
You can cook and Bill does too.
What profitable sharing ☺
The both of you.
You are smart & intelligent,
Put together in every way.
The stylish outfits.

In your house,
Everything has its place.
The Southwest and Indians adorn your life.
Your beautiful Turquoise jewelry
Sits in your front room shadow box.
You gained a solid reputation for home decorating.
How happy I am to have met you,
And be a part of your family.
We are alike in many ways.
Our socks matching our clothes,
Had me laughing for days.
In fact…
We were born on the same day in the month of May,
So I can instantly appreciate,
The strength of your soul,
The work horse effort that leaves us aglow,
Is the pride a Taurus knows.
You've been through a lot,
But your smile shows not an ounce of pain.
It's beautiful and glowing, like a virgin rain,

Lighting up this world like a sunny day.
You are an awesome person in every way.
And Karen, what you did for me...
Blew me away.
The beautiful hat box at Beggars...
Changed my life this day.
I didn't comprehend,
I don't wear hats.
I lifted the lid.
Its empty you said.
Oh, was all I could say.
Confused, I went silent.
Then, your voice. Slowly started. To sink in;
And, when I understood what you had said,
I felt as if I'd been smacked in the head.
The realization largely looming in front of me.
You gave me this hat box for all of my poems –
Find every last one you said, put them in here,
And when this is done,
Your book will be born.
You can do this Debbie.
This is what the hat box is for.

I felt dizzy, with goose bumps,
The light bulb lighting up my brain.
Instantly, I saw it all so clearly.
My holy grail is this hat box.
Sincerely.
I felt I'd been given a 2nd chance in life.
I couldn't wait to get started.
You removed the rose colored glasses from me.

Beyond what words can say.
I saw my plight,
And the whole next year,
Was the best year of my life!
You were right.
My book fell together,
Like it was already planned out.
I knew not what I was doing,
Yet somehow I figured it all out.
The kindness, generosity,
The intuitiveness of your soul to see this in me.
Your magical hat box making it a reality.
I had bits and pieces.
You gave me the dream.
You are my Angel on earth Karen.
My meeting you was meant to be.
You've graced my life.
Immeasurably.
You Karen made "MY JOURNEY IN LIFE" a reality.
You're behind the scenes ability.
You giveth me an empty box;
So filled up.
I'm choked up.
Emotionally.
You bring out the best in me.
I thank you sincerely.
You are very dear to me.
I'm heartfelt for eternity.

ANGELS ON EARTH

Aunt Elly,
You and my Uncle Paul
Were always the greatest
From the time I was small.
You took me and my sister
For weekends quite a lot,
You've taught us many things,
That we've not forgot.
I remember your wooden barrel furniture ☺
We were so impressed.
We felt like we were in a castle,
And tried not to make a big mess.
You taught us how to crochet,
How to knit,
How to make Barbie ponchos
As little kids.
We thought the world of you.
You were here for us in so many ways…
Taught us so many traits.
My 2nd mom and dad.
My heart doth equate.
I remember when Uncle Paul
Got a tumor cut out of his back.
You took the dressing off,
So we could see the big cone hole.
You showed us with your fist,
It almost fit inside this crevice —
It looked so deep and endlessly meaty
That I couldn't comprehend it.

How could there still be more of him
Than that?
I ask.
You loved your husband.
He is so proud, tall, and
Even though he was stricter than hell...
Uncle Paul is now mellow.
You were a great wife,
And a wonderful homemaker you are.

As for being my aunt and Godmother...
I have always held you dear in my heart.
From the very start.
I love you Aunt Elly.
I always have.
I never see you or say it enough,
But I want you to know now,
Having you in my life
Has always made me so very glad.
A smile when I think about you
Is what I always have.
You are courageous,
Very put together.
An entrepreneur in your own right.
You stood on your own.
Handled it all.
Never did you falter.
You only became stronger.
Aunt Elly, I want you to know,
I am in awe of the woman that you are.

ANGELS ON EARTH

My emotions overwhelm me,
And I have to say —
What a gift from God you both are,
And you prove it every day.

Mrs. Jackson,
You've fostered kids,
While you raised your own kids too.
Your heart breaks for all those less fortunate,
I know this is true.

Mr. Jackson,
You ran a driving school,
And taught kid's everyday all you could.
There was always something to learn,
And the learning was always good.

What love and devotion to have in our world today.
You are two people I am thankful for,
And this thought will never go away.

Mr. and Mrs. Jackson,
You are so fine, you blow my mind.
You've raised so many kids,
Be it in driving or at home;
And just when you can call your home your own —
Thinking about how nice it will be —
Just you and the mister —
Once again all alone.

Then...
Your emotions rise.
Your heart breaks open wide.
You put yourselves aside.
You heard about the plight of 3 little boys.
Going to an Orphanage,
To be adopted by different families.

Not only the loss of a mom and dad —
But to never again know the brothers they have.
You and Mr. Jackson make me swell with pride,
For you went and adopted those 3 little boys!

Making sure that all 3 will always be.
You wouldn't let them be ripped apart.
You give them your love, give them your heart,
And give them your home.
All of your lives have been enriched tri-fold,
And never again will they be alone.

Your life is so full.
There is always so much to do.
You are giving these children the best you have.
That's why —
When I think about the Catholic school,
It makes me mad inside!
I understand —
They teach so much more than a regular school can,
Because they include God in their lesson plan.

But...
With Catholic schools being priced so high,
You think they would be honored to give kids a ride.
How could they not provide bus service?
But I think I see...
If they had a bus service,
They could not induce late penalties.

If you don't pick up your children on time,
Even less than 15 minutes late,
You get charged for an hour,
And they think this is fine?

Where is the little bit of charity from their heart,
For the hard working people,
Who want to give their kids the best start?

They constantly have parents on the run;
Especially if you enroll more than one.

This is how I feel and my feelings are real.

But I just don't get some people,
Like that lady from the state,
Who stopped by to see you one day.
She was there to check
On your husband's Drivers Ed Business;
To ensure that everything was up to par, legal and okay.

Instead she gave you the attitude of the day,
Because...

She then saw 3 boys who were not of your race.
She said you were illegally running a day care,
And she felt disgraced,
That you were hiding this from the State.

Mr. Jackson tries to plead —
No way mam these boys are with me.
They are my family.
But she doesn't believe and gets so mad,
That she gives you an attitude,
Like you've never had.

You and Mr. Jackson are so hurt, offended,
And don't understand why,
This lady is acting like you are both slime.

She goes on and on.
I'm sure Mr. Jackson gets a little angry.
She is threating to take away,
The one thing that sustains his family —
His student driver facility.

The sad thing is,
She did succeed,
And took away the business that let you breathe.

It's been a long time — but I hear,
You might get the business back soon.
Mr. Jackson went back to driving for a school.
Sad and hurt,
But hardly wearing a frown.
He would never let his family down.

No matter what comes your way,
Your hearts of gold have never strayed;
And because of this — I know,
It will eventually come back to you tri-fold.
Just like those 3 little boys in tow.
Because — Things happen in 3's — You know.

DELIVERY

DELIVERY

I was walking laps around the pool table at 8:10 am,
When everyone found me.
I looked up and saw my relatives staring at me.
They said are you in labor?
I smiled and said yes indeed!
They jump and panic screaming —
Let's get to the hospital now!
They all start running inside, outside, up and down.
No way, I am feeling okay I said,
As I continued walking around.
How far apart are your pains?
Less than 1 1/2 minutes I said.
They start to plead — Please!
You have waited way too long,
We have to go now,
So the baby isn't born here on the ground!
I finally say okay.
Their annoyances are getting in the way,
Of my feeling tranquil and sound.

We get to the hospital,
I am still big and round.
The nurse tries to put me in a wheel chair,
But I won't sit down —
I am capable of walking around.
They tell me,
I am not allowed to walk any more.
Hospital rules after you're in the door.
They force me into the wheel chair

And push me down the hall —
To the maternity floor.
I hear all these horrific screams bouncing off the walls.
I said what is going on here,
Am I in the psycho ward?
The nurse smiled and said no,
All these women you hear are in labor too.
Gosh what a bunch of wimps I said,
Please take me to my room;
And their screaming is hurting my head!
You won't shut their doors?
Fine — Close mine instead.

This is my 1st time,
And I am so naïve,
That I am caught off guard —
Because a few moments later,
I was louder than anyone on that floor!
Screaming my lungs out, I roared!
Soon after that — My 1st baby was born.
As I lay holding her,
I realize how lucky I am.
My 1st one was like the morning sun.
Only 2 ½ hours of labor,
And now she's in my arms —
The feeling of pain already gone.

Sandy — 9lbs. 7oz 22 inches long.

My 2nd one was a little less fun.
My doctor was on vacation when the time had come.

So the doctor they were giving me,
Already had his own labor patient right down the hall.
Didn't look good for me.
Who was I to compete,
With someone's own personal doctor
Already there for her?
I had to come up with a plan for sure!
I wanted the doctor to take care of me 1st.
What if we both went at the same time?
Would I be left alone to moan?
I didn't like the thought of being 2nd in line,
Or waiting on the side.
I yelled for the nurse.
She came in and checked me.
I was still only dilated to 4.
She then left saying I had a long way to go.
She had to check on those much closer
To being in the delivery room door.

A few minutes later,
I heard a girls screams coming from down the hall,
And it shook me to my core!
What if it was her?
This thought scared me all the more –
So I started to scream like I had never screamed before.
The baby is coming right now! I think it's here;
Hurry come and take care of me!
Oh, why isn't the doctor near…

They rushed into my room –
They didn't even check –

Got me to the delivery room STAT!
And said we're going to wash up,
Be right back.
All of a sudden it was quiet.
I relaxed for a moment feeling good.
Then I realized —
I've only got moments to bring this babe to the outside.
My will took over;
I fought silently and pushed hard.
My baby had no choice now.
I was making her come.
Her time inside me was done.
The doctor and nurses came in,
Delivered my healthy little one.
I felt like I had won.
My will had brought her on.

Laura — 7lbs. 7 1/2oz 18 inches long.
My smallest one, but beautifully done.

A lesson for everyone —
Your will has a strength of its own.
Don't ever feel like you can't push it,
Because it will rise up and take control.
It is always ready to be bold.
So when you think of giving in —
Don't fold and it will take hold.

My 3rd one was such a pleasure to me.
I was more grown up.
I was longing for a boy,

And even though the ultra sound said it was a girl,
I knew in my heart this wasn't true.
I was in labor,
And, my wimpy husband was already crying to me —
We have to go now!
I said no —
I won't go to the hospital to lie in a bed endlessly.
I am going to stay home for as long as I can,
And when the moment is right I will let you in.
But his crying made me feel I was in sin.
So I gave in.
I was in labor forever it seemed.

12 hours later still lying in my hospital bed;
My wimpy husband sleeping now.
I feel as if I'd been had.
The time finally came.
I pushed with all my might!
His head was showing but wouldn't come out.
He was starting to turn a little blue.
They razor sliced me more and more,
This baby needed to fit through my door.
I fought like a caged animal,
Then my boy starts coming out.
The cord is around his neck I shout!
The doctor says it's okay,
The cord is loosely wrapped and not harming his way.
I kept pushing with all my might.
Then my boy came out.
It took 2 doctors to get ahold of him right.
They couldn't believe I had delivered a baby so big.

Without any medicine to comfort me within.
I smiled,
With a baby in me,
I would never allow drugs in my system.
He was a big one and didn't look like a newborn.
I felt so good inside.
He's here.
I finally had my boy.

Tony — 10 lbs. 3oz 24 inches long
A head full of dark hair.
A muscular physique.
Violet eyes.

My son Tom is my youngest one.
Born by cesarean.
My only one — Not rightfully done.
Back to the beginning so you can see,
What happened to him and me.

I was 35 pregnant with my 4th child, older and wise.
I got the birthing room so the whole family could be
A part of this you see.
It was probably my last baby,
And I wanted everyone to share it with me.
My 2 daughters, my husband and my son,
All gathered around waiting for #4 to be born.

It went good but only for so long;
Because then the doctor came in, checked me
And acted like something was wrong.

He said the baby is turned upside down.
I told the doctor to reach in and turn it back around.
He said he couldn't, he had also felt the cord —
The baby's oxygen is being cut off!
We have to do a cesarean right now!
Sign this form on the dotted line please,
So we can proceed.
I pushed the paper away and said No way!
I will have this baby naturally.

My husband broke down,
Sobbing like an emotional wreck.
Scared the kids — they were crying too.
In the end, that's who I gave into.
The crying crew.

As they prepared me for surgery I felt the baby move.
Just as the Anesthelogist was about to administer a shot...
I threw my arms up and yelled stop!
The baby is moving can you see...
Maybe it turned itself around,
Would you check me please?
The Anesthelogist agreed with me,
But then the doctor came in and said there is no time.
He didn't even check me,
And now he had crossed the line...
They put up a sheet so I couldn't see.
I tore it down and said you will hide nothing from me.
They put the sheet back up,
And told me to watch the reflection through the glass.
I laughed.

I ripped the sheet down again and again,
Until they tied my arms to the bed.
You only fueled my fire I said.
I started to fight ridiculously.
They gave me a strong shot, then another one,
And then again and again.
They cannot believe I am still moving around.
They shot me up so much,
They said an elephant would have gone down.
THEN —
They sliced me open and what did everyone see..?
My son came out head first!
He should have been born naturally.

By then I was so out of it,
All those shots finally taking control.
My doctor was beaming and proud.
He hadn't done many cesareans,
And it was his finest moment yet.
I didn't see,
But he punched himself in the shoulder with glee,
And I'll bet thee.
It wasn't a good way for my son to come.
For the next 14 hours I was out of it.
Every time I opened my eyes I would dimly see
My sad family staring at me;
Telling me look at the baby he is right next to you.
I would turn my head to see,
But then my eyes would close,
And that's all I would know.
The instant bond we should have had together,

Took a little long to start.
I felt strange and this comes from my heart.
The doctor later comes in my room looks at me,
Holds up his hands and said...
I thought it was the baby's butt,
Must have been the baby's head.
But I did a great job and you will be pleased,
I promise you will heal nicely.
I feel sick that I gave in to Doctor Prick.
This was the hardest recovery that I ever had.
But my son is healthy, beautiful and for that I am glad.

Tommy – 7lbs. 15oz 20 inches long

On a later note I have to add,
That the doctor who cut me open –
Well at least he wasn't a hack.
I went back into shape and my stomach looked great.
The razor line scar is hardly noticeable,
And I am so glad that he didn't leave me looking bad.
But the final note is...
I was 1 more surgery performed,
And I'll bet that doctor's resume is looking great today.
I feel sorry for the people who also feared...
Because he cut them open too.
I didn't hear this,
I just know it to be true.

DENTAL DEMISE

DENTAL DEMISE

I didn't go to the dentist much when I was young.
My mom tried to keep up on our teeth,
But the wait in the office,
Was too long and no fun.
I feel it bothered me more than some.
Head for the hills my mind kept telling me…
So from then on I learned to say,
My teeth are great!
Nothing wrong here today,
So cancel that appointment;
And I would whine until my mom said okay.

I was naive,
But in my childish mind,
I didn't want to waste my time.

When I was 6,
I dived for a football,
That my dad was going to kick away.

Instead…
My 2 front teeth went flying
When that steel toed boot smacked me in the face!

But I did not cry and I'm not lying.

I smiled even bigger to show I was okay,
And the record –
All I want for Christmas is my 2 front teeth,
Was bought for me that day.

I ran into a wall when I was 15.
Killing my left front tooth,
It turned dark and gray.

What a way to finish out my teens;
But it never stopped me from smiling,
I was reckless but never sad it seemed.

People would say I had a million dollar smile,
Until they saw me in the light of day —
Then my beautiful smile turned them away.
I lost some boyfriends because of this I'd say,
Which hurt,
But I would just smile big and walk away.

When I was 24,
I bit into a big bacon sandwich.
My blackened front tooth stayed,
But my other front tooth cracked in ½ and fell away.
I ran to the dentist right away,
This time determined to sit and stay.

The dentist made a little putty blob,
Adhered it, sanded it and I was on my way.
No dark liquids for 24 hours he said;
But did I listen?
No way!
I had coffee through a straw
The minute I walked in the door.
I thought it would be okay to have a dark drink this way.
But my new piece of tooth turned brown.

Now permanently stained,
And looking worse than my other front gray.
I still finished my 20's with a smile.
No frown in my style.

I made it until I was 44.
And at the top of a cement stairway,
I grabbed on to the collar of my friends big bouncing dog.
Pulled her out, tried to shut the gate;
Her hind legs kicked off the top,
Whipped me around, and pulled me face down
Right into the stairs!

I split my face open in a couple of places,
But it doesn't end there.
My concern was slight.
I am not into hospitals.
I can't stand to sit there all night;
So with butterfly bandages, ice packs and gauze,
I healed my own self,
And except for some scars that I still have today,
6 weeks later the Frankenstein look went away,
And I thought I was okay.
Now 2 years later,
I see what was hidden is coming my way.

The battering of my face hid more than I know.
My teeth are working themselves right out of my mouth,
And in the last 6 months it really shows.

Not to pretty for someone who smiles all the time.

I have 20 teeth left and all but 3,
Are trying to get away from me.

I should have many more,
But every tooth that ached,
Pull it out I would say,
Because I won't come back to sit again
With the same tooth problem.

So here I am,
So excited today!
My boyfriend says it is time,
And he's willing to pay —
No matter how much it is,
Or what it takes...
He wants that beautiful smile back on my face!
So...
Very soon,
My smile will no longer be a disgrace.

For 34 years I have looked this way.
So now you can imagine my excitement today —
And in the waiting room ...
This time I will gladly stay.
I wonder if camping out is okay ☺

MY BEST FRIEND

My boyfriend is my best friend.
We go at it sometimes,
Mostly over my driving and his back seat driving ☺
I can't slow down,
He can't keep quiet.
He thinks he's protecting us,
I think he's nuts;
But we are always lovers —
In the beginning, middle and in the end.

I can't help to touch him and give him rubbings.
I do it without thinking,
And after 11 years my touch he holds dear.

I'm still drawn to his voice,
My hearing finely tuned.
I love the way he sounds...
A deep gravel pitch that gives me chills,
Like no one else I've found.

I love to play with his soft dark hair.
My fingers climbing all over his head...
Then reaching around to his chin,
I find his goatee,
And my fingers again happily sink in.

His brown eyes sparkle with life,
And his smile is twice as nice.
He is aggressive and hyper.

Very honest and forth right,
A stately lion is what he be.
Who takes pride in his den,
Always taking care of his family.

He is Scottish but a lot of Indian I see.
He is built from good stock,
Like the sturdiest of trees.

I feel like the bear,
Rubbing against him constantly.
An itch that never goes away,
I am truly satisfied every day.

He takes care of me so completely,
I couldn't ask for more.
This man is all mine,
And there is no higher score!

We rock at concerts all summer long,
And go skinny dipping in our pool
When nighttime has come.

We are an affectionate couple and people always say...
WOULD YOU GET A ROOM!

We tell them,
Everywhere is our room and anywhere will do –
This room, that room, against the wall...
On the pool table or the front seat of our car.
That desk doesn't look too small;

And the rocking chair?
Well that's a ball!
Except for when my forehead bops off the wall,
And my fingers get pinched against the panel board ☺

We are both a little crazy...
Always laughing,
We have the most fun;
And we always work very hard together,
Making sure that things get done.

This is how I believe it should be
When you truly love someone.

So kudos to my man who is with me still today.

I pray for everyone to find someone;
The magical lock with the matching key.

I feel very blessed that God thought it best,
To bring us both together in this way;
Because we are even happier...
So many years later, down the road today.

ILLNESS

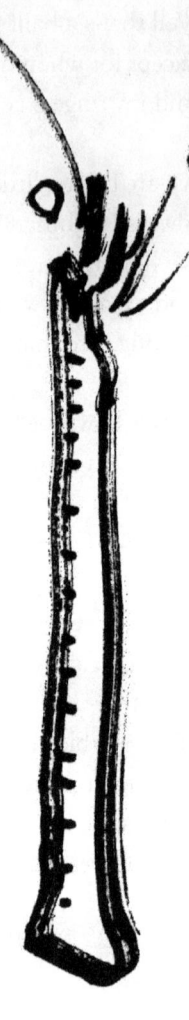

ILLNESS

I weighed 140 pounds since I was 15.
This may sound like a lot,
But I was long, tall, and lean.
Also very active,
I was muscular and fit.
I enjoyed being a tomboy;
Playing basketball, catching snakes, throwing rocks,
Skipping stones, climbing trees, riding a dirt bike
Was great fun for me.
The boys in the neighborhood liked me because,
I wasn't afraid to get roughed up or dirty.
But...
I grew up in a physical family.
It was my dad's greatest pride,
To be the hardest worker he could,
And we grew up working by his side.
Long into adulthood,
People are surprised to find out how much I weigh.
At carnivals I always won that prize I'd say.

I still feel so young on the inside, healthy and strong.
I'm 49 and haven't changed those ways.
My mind doesn't compute age,
And getting up in your days.

Then 3 months ago something went wrong.
My stomach blew out,
Like I was being pumped up with an air gun.
Filling me up to my neck and chin.
It seemed like in a matter of days I gained 22 pounds.

I ran to the doctor in January, only to hear her say...
A Thyroid problem is what's wrong with me today.
Oh!
And not just today, but for the rest of my life!
They tell me exercise will never help me alone,
But with an everyday pill, from now until forever
Will put me in the right zone,
And that eventually I'll even out.
Man I am freaking out!

All of a sudden I look my age.
I'm just a squared middle aged lady
Who is coveringup the grays.
This is not okay.
I can't even dress cute anymore.
My boyfriend has been wonderful
And that's my only high score,
Because the rest of me feels defeated —
What a blow to my core.

And now...
Spring is in the air.
Should I even care?
My Thyroid is out of control.
It's not the losing weight kind you know.
I am not feeling pretty, or thin, or at ease.
It sucks to be me right now.
I'm just feeling tired these days.
Where is the hip hip hurrah and hooray?
The sun is out but I don't want to play.
Not today.

In any case my spirit has high hopes,
Even though my body says nil.
But, when my spirit wins out —
This belly will not be a hill!
It feels better to be fit.
I hope I make it before summer time hits.
This is when I feel the most alive and in my glory,
And I'll be damned
If I will wear clothes that hang on me neatly —
No! That's not the end of my story.
I'm betting I can end it petit Ely,
My mind is thinking discreetly.

Yes, spring is in the air.
Time to shed this thick skin,
And let out the butterfly within.
Because, I am in there,
And I will emerge somewhere I swear!
Realistically though…
Maybe not this year.

It is now June, they have upped my medicine.
Mentally I am feeling better,
But still blowing up like a balloon.
It has been 6 months now,
And I am starting to realize,
That no ending is coming soon.

My spirit is still fighting,
I am trying hard not to let it go —
But for all the people out there who have this, they know.

I am fighting a battle within myself.
In the end one of us has to go.
I'd like to take this Thyroid,
And rip it right out of my throat!
This is just my silly sad thinking – I know.
Everyone loves Deb I've heard so many people say...
But now, my emotional attitude gets in the way.

I don't understand...
If a pill is supposed to give me back what I am missing;
Why am I still so out of hand?
I am determined to take command,
But keep getting lost in a jam.
That tunnel looks so long and I can't see,
Where the light is at the end of this for me.
Realistically I know the light is no longer there.
I have to find my own way through the dark.
If there is a door hidden somewhere –
I'll find it I swear!

So like I said this year is a bust.
But my hopes are high for next year...
I have to believe –
I have to trust –
And above all I can't ever give up!
I will flick off that doubt
Like a mosquito full of my blood...
It got a piece of me,
But then I squashed it as hard as I could
Until it didn't exist anymore.
I believe – my will is this good.

ILLNESS

Barbra,
Oh Barbie I am so sad.
I heard you were ailing,
And it might be bad.

Whatever you do,
Don't ever give up hope.
Our spirit is the biggest drive in healing ourselves,
I've learned to take note.

We have to turn to doctors too,
Because they do all the things that we can't do.

Like a burn,
You have to heal from the inside out;
And I'm praying that every last one of those
Little F**kers
Just plum tire out —
Dissolve —
Go away.

Get the f**k out of my cousins body!
I want to yell and say.
I love you Barbra.
I hope you'll be ok.

ILLNESS

Hey Colleen,
Just thinking about you.
Sorry to hear about all you've been through.
That is such a major loss I tell you.
I'm sure it's devastating and hard to break away,
From holding on to some negative emotions still today.

We were such a hardy steadfast bunch.
We would never believe that things like this
Would happen to us when we grew up.
We were all rowdy and strong,
Nothing could keep us down,
Our spirit and our will always kept us moving on.

We are all grown up now our lives doing okay —
Then out of the darkness tragedy starts to prey,
And one day when we wake up nothing is ok.
Something not just slightly wrong —
Life altering in every way.
We are sickened and it's hard to believe,
That this would ever happen to you or me.
Our belief in our insides plays a big part of our healing.
Our inner strength will get us through any dealing —
But sometimes we can't stop reeling on the inside.
Anguish cannot be denied.
Somehow eventually we will get past it even if we like it none.
We are stuck with what has happened.
What's done is done.

I am still fighting a demon right now too;
And for the first time — EVER!
I've learned what it's like to lose your will.
The thought that I learned this
Freaks me out to this day still!
I have good moments but also a lot of days bad.
Suddenly it's hard not to be negative.
Before I only knew how to be happy.
Now and sometimes often I only know how to be sad.
AND IT MAKES ME SO MAD!

This is not who we are Colleen...
So let's make a pact (you & me) to never give up —
No matter how much our emotions bleed —
Let us always believe we were meant to be,
And f**k any sickness
That makes us feel less than deserving.
Our fights show we are worthy,
Our desire is still burning.
Our hearts may ache,
But it's simply just a part of life we have to take.

Let's keep hoping for the best,
And let's deal with the worst.
Let's believe we will always survive,
That it was instilled in us from birth.

And the one day when we are truly not meant to be,
I hope we accept it gracefully;
But until then we are still here.
Let's hold on to our being precious and dear.

I love you girl,
My childhood growing up friend.
Let's toast too many more good times,
And pray for the bad ones to end.

Let's send the ugliness straight back to Hell,
Where it can dwell.
Though we have felt it well —
It has no future up here,
And we know this Colleen,
Because we have lived to tell;
So in my opinion —
This time —
We have beaten Hell.

ILLNESS

I am sending a card to your demons inside –
R.I.P Cancer, I hope you die!
Don't you have anything better to do
Than to feed on the meager
Trying so hard to get through.

My girlfriend is not deserving of this,
So hit the road or the skies –
I don't care how you get out,
As long as Diane stays alive.

You are the devil clinging to her insides!
Her breasts are not free room and board
For your tumors and cysts –
You should be ashamed of yourself you filthy slime,
How dare you exist!
Stop rotting her insides.
Spread your cancer around in Hell.
This is the only place where you may dwell.

You want to be so devastating and bad?
PROVE IT –
Come on the outside and let's get down,
Give her a fighting chance to take you on.

YOU ARE A F**KING WUSS!
I didn't think you would.
You only know how to hide –
But Diane is a strong girl,
And she will fight you all the way down the line.

You are also hitting her wallet,
But that's okay —
Because she will pay to have you erased today!

Next party — 666 Devils way.
That is where Cancer can eternally play.
In us it must stay away.
Diane I beg this for you today;
And I will kneel down and pray.

ILLNESS

Larry our beloved friend,
I cannot believe that something like this
Has happened again...
To our buddy, our pal, our very best friend!
We love you man.
Don't know why once again
You were dealt this raw hand.
And now...
The grueling work ahead for you,
Is making that left side remember how to move.
Even right now though you're feeling slack,
Your will is strong,
It can outlast,
Any short coming
Any obstacle
Any block in the path
Any setback.
You can do this Larry,
We all want you back.
Your time is right now — right here!
Time to shine,
Time to persevere!
Work hard and make yourself well.
Stomp out all that is scarier than Hell.
You haven't understood your plight.
Why do bad things happen to us?
Is it wrong?
Is it right?
You may not be deserving of this;

But now with no choice,
You have to move in a different direction —
Take an alternate plan of action.
You've been given a second chance at life.
It comes with some setbacks,
And now regulations apply.
You can't anymore get yourself kicked out of the game —
You have to now follow the rules,
Even if they are lame.

So — DROP AND GIVE ME 50!
Because this many more years
We want you to remain.
We're pulling for you Larry!
We're cheering in the stands!
We're ganging up to oust this sickness,
So sickness — get the Hell out of my friend!
He is a great man and has no time
To deal with your unworthy slime!
To the hospital I wanted to Fed Ex this,
But Jimmy Johns was the quicker man.
I hitched a ride with them,
And here I am
At the hospital w/ poem in hand.
Oops — silly humor sneaking in again;
But what is not silly is your life man.
It's important to all of us, especially you.
Larry, how can you do anything else?
You can't my friend — life is the only choice.
I beg of you to understand.
Your boys want you home Dad.
How can you argue with that?

COLIC

Sandy —
My beautiful lioness so strong and proud.
You were my 1st baby,
And my you were loud.
They called it colic,
But to me —
You screamed in agony.
Crying 18 hours a day —
There was no medicine,
No relief —
I tried everything I believe,
But no cure came our way.
So I just sat and cried with you every day.

I wouldn't let anyone else babysit you,
And no one else could really hold you.
The stress they showed —
Showed me,
That I was the only one with the durability.

Family parties didn't go well —
And I wasn't going to hide away with you in a back room,
So that everyone else could enjoy the parties guilt free,
Of having to hear my baby scream.

It only took 1 time —
I packed you in the car and took you home.
I didn't want you to see that others couldn't handle you…

So for the next few months,
It was just you and me.

I was very protective of you
Like a mother lion with her cub.
My claws were out constantly
When someone suggested that we should stop by.
I would say no thank you,
And in the back ground...
I would hear my family or friends cry.

I know they loved us,
But I wasn't yet willing to give anyone a try.

The first 6 months of your life...
Took 5 years off of mine.

And just when I thought there was no end in sight –
Out of the blue...
One morning when you woke up,
Something was new.
It took me a while to realize –
There were no tears in your eyes.

You were smiling, happy and you did not utter 1 cry –
Ever again I would almost have to say;
Because from that morning on,
Your happiness stayed.

You grew up to be a beautiful young lady,
So caring and fine.

People and kids are drawn to you —
You have the biggest heart and charm that does not stop.

People are always surprised,
That such a beautiful girl can be so kind and wise.
But it never went to your head or got in your way.
You've stayed that same wonderful girl,
That you are today.

Of course —
Only after the first 6 months went away.
Sorry girl it's the truth.
But I can also say,
You made me love children.
You are the biggest part of who I am today.

SELF WORTH

SELF WORTH

Laura, Laura,
Where do I start?
You are such a good girl,
And you have the biggest heart.
You are so kind and giving in so many ways,
Don't chastise yourself,
Because you are definitely okay.
You have the greatest smile, the nicest hair,
Your personality deserves an Oscar – and –
I know everyone would applaud you there.
Your stamina is proven,
You are upbeat, never down.
You have so much charisma you could light up a town.

So sit down with that thinking frown;
You just need to open that heart up,
Let those boys in past the surface.
It's the only thing you are missing,
You silly little elf.
You need to remember
You are a beautiful girl with lots of appeal.
So, don't be a stranger in your relationships.
Allow yourself to feel.
Your headache will heal.
You are still so young with a long life ahead,
Believe in others fair maiden, you've nothing to dread.

I know your history,
Of putting your dad's face on your boyfriends isn't pretty;

But let go of the past honey,
And the future can be sunny.
Don't equate everyone
With his mistakes.
It's not their fault,
And it's not a fair start.
Focus your drive
On what you see in the person by your side.

Because of what was,
Don't let it be what will be.
You can change it now don't you see?
It doesn't take much to let the sun fill your sky.
Come on Laura; fill up their self-worth with pride.
Let them know you on the inside.
Let them capture this beautiful butterfly.

God will always be holding your hand.
Believe in him,
Because he is the one
Who truly has your front, back and side.

Through Jesus we learn what happiness is really about;
So let go of that doubt.
Though God understands our doubting ways,
He will always stick with us,
And if we allow him —
He will help us through our haze.

He is the true believer no matter what we do.
And if you acknowledge you need his help,
He will come through for you in ways you will not believe.

But you will see.
Believe me.

Because not only do I believe in you —
God has always believed in you.
This I know to be true;
And…Our love is endless for you.

SELF WORTH

Ashley,
It is true.
You are having a baby,
And yes I am happy for you.

Now you know what you must do —
The pills of choice from here on in,
Are prenatal vitamins for you and the little one within.

I believe this baby is a blessing in disguise.
This little boo boo is going to help you
Become healthy, happy and wise.

Everything happens for a reason,
And sometimes — right away we don't know why.
But God is watching over you,
And his eyes are lit up with joy.
Sometimes in order to save a soul —
Another soul will provide,
The strength and will for you to succeed;
Because from now on
Your heart will abound
Endlessly with love
For this little one
By your side.

You are already a world wiser,
This I can see,
And I think it is so beautiful that you will be,
Forever loved by this little entity endlessly.

Believe me Ashley,
No matter what doubts you have,
Your heart will soar,
The day of delivery,
When you are given this baby…
To hold ever more.
With tears of joy I thank you for this soon to be,
New addition to the Buchanan family!
I love you Ashley.
I wish for happiness to come your way and stay.

SELF WORTH

Jen — I am writing to you because I see,
That you are too mentally heavy.
You've weighed your mind down with so much stuff;
Your brain is over full and will not shut.
You need to get rid of this junk.

Jen — I knew you...
Hyper, happy and full of life.
Now you are quiet and still,
This isn't right.

Being the youngest one,
Life felt centered around you.
But when it's time to grow up...
Some don't want to —
Some don't know how to —
And some don't get why they should have to.
But you cannot change what life is all about.
Eventually we are on our own,
Trying for ourselves to figure it out —
Whether we like it or not.
And this next stage in life...
Is vital for the young adult.
Much like the womb from which we were brought.

Oh —
There are holes in the ground along the way.
We've all fallen into them and yes it is dismay.
We finally felt experienced,

But are now the green horns again starting out.
But we become stronger.
That's what makes us who we are today.
So — you can enjoy life's ride and also fall into a hole.
But, when you can pick your own self up,
Your insides will glow.

Everyone is always here for you,
Even if you think not.
It is hard for us to kick the young ones out of the nest —
But we are always here for you when we feel its best.
We can't help but to soothe the ruffled feathers,
Although we will still send you home
With a smile and a kiss on the head.

We are your moral support and we love you,
Now go back home to your own bed.
Sometimes it's good to sleep on it somebody said.

Jen — You are such a good girl,
You just need to turn some things around.
Your thoughts are still young so I won't put you down;
But I will be honest.
I just want to help you come around.

Jen — I watched you eating a while back.
Stop shoveling in the snacks.
You get no help from them — no way.

Jen — Drinking hard liquor
Is somthing you should not do.

I'm sure it brings you up at first,
Making you feel good too.
But the downfall to liquor,
Is in the end, it leaves you feeling blue
The more you drink,
The more down in the dumps you'll be.
Try a mixed drink if you don't like beer,
But stay away from the hard liquor, it's full of despair.

Jen — What you are doing is not ok.
You are bottling up your emotions inside...
Holding on to anger and doubt,
Letting none of it slide.
You are freaking out your insides.
Your mind in too much overtime.
Don't be resentful and hold things in,
When you do that you never can win.
Trying to be something your not —
Will leave you mentally stressed,
Staying full of doubt,
And emotionally tied in a knot.
Stop trying so hard to be approved.
Just being yourself naturally will work best for you.
Take a walk at least once a day.
Let your thoughts wander but not stray.

Jen — As much as you are missing your mom,
She is missing you too.
She was crying to me saying how she hardly talks to you.
She so want's to have a great relationship with you,
And believe it or not, Joel is here for you,

And brother Christopher too.
You don't ever need a reason to call...
Just saying I love you says it all.

You need to start filling your self-worth with pride.
You've had some ups and downs but honey —
Life has not passed you by.
You are still a young girl,
And for you the world is opened wide.

Jen — They say it is darkest before the dawn.
If you hang in there long enough,
What's missing will be found.
Don't worry so much about everyone else.
Time to start setting yourself straight.
Learn to love yourself.
Accept who you are.
Good or bad ways?
Everyone has them.
We all deal with the bad,
Try to work on them a little too.
But we are who we are,
And I like who you are Jennie Boo.
Don't forget to always talk to God.
He'll help along the way,
And I swear you'll feel him there.
With conviction this I can say.
Don't try so hard Jen.
Just be you ☺ okay?

Jen — it's okay to feel awkward right now;
Like in your own family you don't fit in —
But there is no room for another Jen.
We all love you honey.
Open your heart and feel it from within.

Jen — I felt I was the black sheep in my family too.
I spent a good part of my growing up life
Feeling just like you.
I was awkward and blurted dumb things out.
I never thought I was as smart or as cute as someone else.
But deep down —
I still liked myself and who I was.
Sometimes it just takes a while to realize who you are;
And everyone is great in their own way.
Let yours SHINE and you'll be on your way.

Stomp the animosity out!
There is no longer room for that part.

We've now filled this space with the sun,
And it is ready to help you bloom...
Like a beautiful summer flower in the middle of a field.
It feels lost and closed off —
But to all the birds, butterflies and insects,
They see nothing else;
Except for this beautiful blossom sitting there by itself.
You are never really alone.

Jen — Please lighten your load.

You are too young to feel so old.
Take every day as it comes
And it won't be long before you see
The path that lay out in front of you.
Stretching endlessly.

Jen — And in the end if I could say nothing else...
We lost our Christopher,
And if he would of waited just a little while longer —
Everything would have worked itself out.
He'd be driving a car, having a job,
While learning to rebuild transmissions
For his dad, no doubt.
He would have been awesome at that.
The Lego King!
The guy who could put together anything!

He would have been such a kick ass grownup,
So tall and proud;
But now our hearts endlessly bleed through.
A big gaping hole that can never be patched.
I'm telling you true.
The finality is so surreal.
And the worst part about it is —
It's a done deal.
There can be no appeal.

Jen — Whatever you think...
Don't ever think about giving up.
You are worth way too much.
Relax some and let yourself grow up.

Look – the sun is smiling at you.
Can you feel its warm touch?
Love life Jen.
It offers so much.

SELF WORTH

I met a lady today,
Whose ex-husband has abused her in some way.
She is jumpy, skittish and giggles
To hide her insecurities.
And Barbra,
When you did tell me that you were previously abused
Well —
I could already see that in you.
I don't know what you've been through,
Or what went down...
But thankfully you're alive.
The abuse in the past,
Can no longer hurt you now.
You are a strong woman.
Just mentally down,
And you won't feel great over night;
Time is the only thing
That will calm you down.
You are beautiful and sweet.
Did not deserve to be beat.
We get so caught up in only what we know.
Hanging in too long —
Which is the death of many women statistics show.
You are one of the lucky ones.
You made it out — you know.
Don't let it ruin the rest of your life.
Props we don't want to give
To someone nastier than slime.
A person void of compassion, brain and mind.

Too gross to even step on.
Wears a mask all the time.
Let's work on getting this ugliness shredded,
Until it is a mere dust particle
Not visible to the human eye.
Not even seen inside.
And, you should actually feel so damn good,
Because Barbra…
You've already done the biggest thing of all —
You walked away from all that's a horror.
You didn't go back and that's the first step.
You are stronger now because of it.
Confidence can again settle in;
And look what's happened since then.
You now have a good honest man.
No tin foil here. The halo is real.
Let his gentle ways lead you.
You will feel secure and in control again.
Don't harbor the bad.
Don't let it nest within.
Clean out those rotten eggs.
Lay them to rest.
Let the devil claim them;
And let the new you in the new nest
Begin a new life down a different path.
One that is filled with happiness.
You no longer have nothing to dread.
You can now look ahead
And hold your head up high.
So bring that beautiful smile forward.
Let the sun shine through your eyes.

This next chapter is all you.
You've already done your time.
And now it's time for you to shine.
I know you'll do just fine.

SELF WORTH

Precious.
My dear Precious.
I don't know how to begin or what to say.
I am at a loss for words,
Because no matter what I say...
The demon that hurt you — I cannot change or take away.
But I feel compelled to talk to you anyway.

Precious — You were burned and scarred
By a selfish, gross, disgusting,
Immature f**k of a person in life —
Someone that shouldn't be allowed to be alive right now —
The worst kind of coward —
One that can't be called human —
A filthy — slimy — mauling animal
That should have been shot on sight,
And then shot over and over again
Just to make sure he cannot ever come back to life!

Precious — You were abused in the worst way possible.
You brutally learned things you shouldn't ever know.
I know a piece of you has died,
That your heart is now lost,
That you relive the nightmare,
That you are left feeling cold —
The innocence of a child now seems so long ago.
Who are you now?
When you are so young but feeling so old.
Who now could you possibly be — ?

You don't fit either of those molds.
My sweet child,
For you, life has taken its toll.

Most will say the worst is over,
But I know that that's not so.
The mind rolls on and on.
That jagged crevice looms large
Creating an awful deep hole.
It's like you've fallen to your death and survived,
Because you are still
Emotionally bruised and battered on the inside.

I know you are sickened in your heart;
And it's okay to feel lost and angry,
And it's okay to feel like you are falling apart,
And it's okay not to understand
The horrible blow of this life's dealt hand.
And it is alright to mourn for yourself and your loss…
This is how we slowly heal Precious.
We don't ever forget.
But we do slowly move forward.
1 foot in front of the other.
1 step at a time.

I don't think you can ever figure out
The sickness in someone else's mind –
The one who bears no heart.
But what you truly need to believe and know
Is that you never did anything wrong Precious.
I swear this on my soul.

I know there are still tears in your eyes.
Why do bad things happen?
I'm sorry Precious,
I don't have an answer as to why.

But Precious I do know,
You cannot let the rest of your life go by.
Sometimes it feels like giving up is the way to go — ,
But Precious the answer is NO!!!
NO! NO! NO! HELL NO!
Don't ever again feel like it is okay for us to lose you.
Please — I am begging you — Please
Don't ever again think this way.
There is a reason you are here...
You were meant to stay alive —
To live long and become wise.
Don't give up on the future honey,
There is still so much for you to do.
An endless path is waiting to lead you.

Your mom, dad and grandparents love you,
And your brothers and sisters — well — their ok.
Just kidding ☺ I know they love you.
I just thought I'd throw a smile your way;
Because brothers and sisters
Can be a pain in the neck sometimes I'd say.

Precious — you need to watch the movie
(It's a Wonderful Life)
From beginning to end.
I know you are young,

But what you will see is
That you don't even realize how many other lives
Have been touched by you yourself,
By just being alive;
And all of these hearts Precious don't ever want yours to fold.
The final grief is the most unbearable.
The card no one ever wants to touch or hold.

You have such a good mind and a strong will.
Just keep moving forward Precious.
I promise —
Eventually you will get over that hill
And be glad you made it to the other side.
It will feel great to be a part of life,
With the sun shining in the sky.
A soft breeze moving your hair about your face.
A fat fuzzy caterpillar sitting on a railing,
His sticky legs keeping him in place;
And the birds make noise as they pass by.
Oh Oh — I hear your dog barking.
He wants to go outside...
You can stop reading now and go do that,
I'll wait patiently until you get back by.

Just kidding silly.
My humor is sometimes —
Well it's just who I am,
I don't know why.

Precious — You know me.
I am not a doctor or a therapist.

I am just a simple person with a heart
That wants to help you not to fall apart.
There is no designated healing time,
And sometimes it takes a while
Before you can take it away from the forefront
And put it to the back of your mind,
And I swear Precious this will happen with time.
Discouragement is okay —
But it is not worthy of being the final thought of the day.

The million hearts around you, who love you
Don't ever want to see you go —
Unless you move out
Because you are getting married you know ☺
I love you Precious — no rash decisions ok?
Just take it slow and let the healing start to grow.
It will
Bloom inside you again.
This I know.
We all love you heart and soul.
Precious...
I want you to know.

YOUNG LOVE

YOUNG LOVE

When I was young,
My sister Tami and I
Always went camping with my grandma and grandpa.
It was the most fun and for the biggest part,
I loved being young.

My gram and gramp belonged to a group
Called Skid Row Camp.
There was always a reason or a theme,
And we would ever faithfully
Do the (Hoe down square dance) to end the evening.
On our Hawaiian luau we wore lei's and grass skirts.
We cooked our food in the ground.
I was a little unsure about eating somthing
That was buried in the earth;
But the steamy tin foil wraps they pulled out —
Turned out to be delicious no doubt.

In the wilderness,
I learned to make sponge candy w/ my Grammy.
Hobo popcorn —
Sitting around a campfire
With tinfoil, popcorn, and a stick.
It was always a little burned,
But I loved it and couldn't wait for my turn.

My grandma and grandpa taught me a lot.
The outside was also their favorite spot.
How to find your way back,

How not to get lost,
Always stay on the path,
Don't wander off.
What plants to touch,
What plants you cannot,
Don't ever go out alone after dark.

On some evenings,
Everyone gathered to watch a movie
That was set up outside.
These were the best of times.
One night on our way to the movie site —
My sister and I
Saw a brown bear stretching on a tree close by.
My sister was scared, but not I.
It was kind of cool and creepy, all at the same time.
He never really looked our way —
But my sister was done for the day.
She ran home —
Wouldn't stay to watch the show.
I was mad because with her I had to go.
So — I also missed the show.
But that was only 1 out of the many that we saw.
I loved this existence.
It was unrivaled by far.
In my eyes my grandma and grandpa were the stars.

They always did so much with us,
I am blessed couldn't ask for more,
And I wouldn't change a thing that's for sure.

One day while camping we were having a contest
To see who could collect the most pop tabs.

My sister and I set out walking through the woods.
We had gotten some but not a lot;
Then out of nowhere this boy walked up,
Said his name is Bill and asked if he could join us.
My sister whispered to me…
He's going to steal our tabs,
And I said don't worry, if anything —
We'll gang up and take his 1st.

Out loud — My sister said, No Way!

Out loud — I said yes, okay.

He grabbed my hand and we started walking.
I don't know when my sister left.
I was enjoying the time with my new found friend.
We talked, walked and laughed forever it seemed.
I was 11 and this was the 1st time…
I realized I had different feelings.

Suddenly it was dark.
Where had the day gone?
I have been out since late morning,
I realized with a start —
Creeping in is the feeling of forlorn.

We said goodbye.
I ran back to my camp.

It was our last night there and...
My gram, gramp and sis seemed a little mad;
But I clowned my way out of it like I always have.
I woke up early the next morning.
Couldn't wait to get outside.
I knew we were leaving soon.
I wanted to find Billy.
Tell him goodbye.

I never did find him.
My heart a little heavy on the home ride.

5 weeks later...
During a family picnic
At my Aunt Laverne's and Uncle Ed's,
We were playing tag
And running around their huge backyard
When...
The children next store came out of their house
And asked if they could join us.
I froze in my steps and stared.
Billy was one of the kids that lived there.
My eyes lit up and my smile grew wide,
Instantly I felt so happy inside.
Our eyes locked forever it seemed.
Neither of us moving;
Until we heard everyone scream —
We're playing dodge ball you dope's,
Would you get in your spot!
We both started laughing and joined the crowd.

Later on playing tag...
We wrestled each other to the ground
Laughing and play fighting
When I realized my heart started to pound.
We both stopped wrestling and stared each other down.

Time to go my dad yelled and we piled back into the car.
Can we come back here again tomorrow?
My mom turned around and gave me a strange look.
The kids next store are cool I said.
I would like to hang out with them again.
No my parents said and that was the end of that.

I was feeling so elated and now I'm feeling mad...
But Halloween is coming soon;
And I secretly smiled —
Knowing the exact day that I would be back.

On Halloween day we trick or treated around our blocks,
Then at my urging —
My mom pulled up in front of my Uncle Ed's house.
We all got out and they ran to the 1st house.
It wasn't the way I wanted to go so...
I was heading opposite.
My mom yelled stop!
You all stay together or get back in the car.

This way I yelled and kept moving on.

Billy was in the middle of a Boy Scout meeting
When we came to the door.

Trick or Treat we said!
Our eyes fell on each other,
And we didn't see anything more;
Until his mom came to the door and said —
Oh there you are!
What are you still doing here outside?
Go back to your meeting — remember its inside,
And didn't you already give some to them?
Give me that basket and I'll hand the candy out.
Bill said — our meeting is done.
His mom said — no it's not.
Everyone had ran off ahead,
So I reluctantly left;
But before I was completely out of his yard
I turned around and looked back.

He was still standing on the porch.
I smiled as I walked to the next house.

The next year on Halloween
In Midlothian and Crestwood,
They banned Trick or Treating.
Instead —
They threw a Halloween bash at St Chris.

I couldn't wait to be done Trick or treating in Oak Forest.

The time finally came to go.
I was so excited and my anticipation surmounts...
But when we got there and walked in the door —
My jaw dropped!

So many people everywhere —
It was a little intimidating trying to move in there.

It took a good part of the evening,
But I finally found Bill behind a stockade of long tables.
He was running a game or something back in there.
We locked eyes smiled and said hi.
Then some adult yelled —
Get over here boy!
Billy said I'm working got to go — bye.
Just like that he walked away,
And I was left wishing I hadn't come to St Chris today.

Many years later in the summer when I was 18,
My girlfriend Donna and I
Walked to the carnival in Midlothian.
We were having a blast walking around,
When out of no where
Somebody grabbed me and turned me around.

Billy? I said.
That name now long out of my head.

He hugged me smiled and laughed.
Gave me a stuffed animal that he had won,
Grabbed my hand and started to walk around.
I felt a little strange.
I was a different person now.
I let go of his hand smiled and said,
My girlfriend and I are going over there,
But it was really nice seeing you — take care.

I walked away and left him standing there.
I felt a little guilty and sad,
But after almost 6 years —
Just a child hood memory is what I have.

I ran into him again
Right before the carnival was to end.
I realized I was still excited to see him —
My heart was pounding.
He and his friends offered Donna and me a ride home.

Are you just going to drop us off I said?
With a smile he said yes — right at your door,
I promise you fair maiden,
Then he gave me a little bow.
How very chivalrous I said with a smile,
But on the inside I was thinking all the while...

He wasn't asking me to hang out.

He was asking to drop us off.

No thanks I said, we'd rather walk.

I am now 27 and was hanging out with my mom one day.
She said she was going to visit an elderly lady,
Check up on her and make sure she's okay.
Did I want to come with her?
I said yes I'm not doing anything today.

Imagine my surprise —
The house we pulled in front of...
Was the house that Billy had grown up in.
I felt the same old excitement stirring in me again.

Grandma is the only one who lives there now.
No sign of anyone else around.

I saw Billy's picture on the wall.
Inquired about him,
And grandma said he's married now,
But he's having some problems.
Don't know how it's going to go.
I don't get around much you know.

After our visit was done and we were pulling away,
My happy thoughts kept coming about how lucky I was
To have experienced this kind of love
When I was so young.
I don't think we ever even kissed.
Our love was pure, beautiful and innocent.
My very 1st love.
I feel blessed.

YOUNG LOVE

Shae,
I'm really pissed off at Sam and I want to say,
That I don't like him today.
What a jag off to treat you this way.

You never asked for much,
But got not even a card on Valentines day
Even though you were hurt, you dealt with it.
You put up with his downfalls and believed
His heart was in the right place.
Just a job is all he needs.

But the sad fact in life is that
He is not worth your strife.

Sam is basically a good guy and you've had lots of fun.
He has helped you climb the ladder
And you are starting to feel the sun.
Not by choice — you had to,
Because he doesn't get things done.
Now you notice he is stuck back on a rung.
You caught him messing around with someone!

So F**K THE LOW LIFE SCUM BAG
That you've taken a liking to!
You have had a couple of years together,
But life is not through with you.
There is so much more to see and do.
You are a beautiful young lady, although a little angry,

And maybe you deserve to be.
You are going to school and working,
So forget that Drone bee! Who is not even a worker.
Next Please.

You deserve to be taken care of properly.
So don't let go of that just yet,
Until you find a man who can take command –
Treat you in all the right ways;
And at the very least tell you sometimes...
How much you brighten up his days.

So... Do not dismay Lassie.
I swear the right man will come along,
And fill your heart with love and praise.

Don't settle for less.
You are no second fiddle,
You are 1st class.
You deserve the right babe –
And when you find him, your home will be made.

Don't get so down when you are young.
Life is all about having fun,
Paying your bills,
Vacationing in the sun.
There is so much more for you hon.
Just let him go and be done.

Afterword...
Shae did let him go and for 6 months he was gone.

But — Sammy did come through,
Got a job, an apartment and his girlfriend back too.
We are proud of you Sammy.
This is what you needed to do.
Just don't forget to show your love too.

Closing —
Sad to say, it ended anyway;
But they remain very good friends to this day;
It takes time to find your way in life,
And I am sorry for being a Meany,
Because Sam, with his genuine heart and soul,
We have learned to love completely.

DRIVING w/ me

Prologue,
On the way to the shop one day,
Todd screamed at me —
SLOW DOWN!
Do you even realize how fast you are going?!
The chill of realization went through me.
No I said, I never look at the speedometer,
Unless I think I am going too slow,
And then I can't stop staring at it.
But, I don't try to drive fast,
I just like to get where I'm going.
I dropped him off at the shop,
And ran down the street to my doctor appointment.
While in the waiting room
I wrote this next poem on the back of my receipt.

DRIVING W/ ME

I don't try to drive fast.
I just like to get where I'm going.
I like my wheels in motion,
The speedometer humming.
A terror I can be —
If you are driving too slow in front of me.
I'll ride your ass,
You'd better get out of my way fast!
And if you are on the phone,
I am coming at you like Al Capone!
I'll drive into the meridian, or off on the side,
And scare you while I get out in front of you,
Getting realclose to your ride.
I have my own set of rules for driving,
But I can usually chill;
If I'm the first one at the stoplight,
Or getting all greens
I'm happier still.
So...
Give me the road,
And give me my space —
Stay out of my lane.
Stay out of my way.
I only brake for animals,
Not automobiles
I'd say.

DRIVING W/ ME

The light turned green.
I counted to 15.
Then I started...Laying on my horn.
Not to be mean,
But to make others acknowledge the green.
My boyfriend starts to scream —
ARE YOU FRIGGING CRAZY!
HOW DO YOU DARE!
THAT IS A COP IN FRONT OF YOU!
And I say...
I don't care who is in front of me on the road;
The light is green and it's time to go.
BEEP! BEEP! BEEP!
Don't be slow.
We're not walking, we're driving you know.
It's sometimes hard to deal with people every day.
Why some bother getting into a car well...
I don't know what to say, except that it is not okay.
It is not okay to finally get up to speed
When the next light is already there.
3 blocks and still can't reach 45?
To me is a schiesty dive.
Who would take so long to get up to speed
And still drive slow?
A battering ram is what I need!
And...this thought...makes me smile...endlessly.
To move cars away! YES!
I'll slide them with ease,
Then stepping on the gas would be up to me,

And not all those others
Driving foolishly slow on the road unwilling to go.
But...
When I'm around they'll learn to know —
If you don't step on the gas off you'll go.
I'll push you right out to the side.
Are you feeling lucky?
Will it be grassy, or a steep incline?
Are you out of your mind!
Do you really want to mess with me?
Because...
I won't care where you end up —
As long as, I have the lead.

DRIVING W/ ME

I don't know why, when I drive,
I feel like a race horse
Determined to quickly finish my course.
The fastest time ever!
(I think about this so much)
I set my own time limits.
Hate when it's a bust.
Then I get stuck at a light...
My race horse nerves start jumping inside.
Getting ready to leave the gate;
I am antsy, jittery, my foot shaking to go!
My anticipation surmounting...
This red light seems so slow.
Waiting for the relief,
My body wants so bad to meet.
That green light is my lifted gate.
To pounce across the intersection,
I cannot wait.
Once again,
I need my space.
Need to calm down.
My heart doth race.
I must have been
A race car driver
In a previous life;
Or a horse, a crazy Ancestor,
Or maybe, just running for my life!
I could have been a small time animal
Not willing to be something's dinner tonight.

Thoughts of why I need to go are endless,
So... why question it.
Does it matter where it came from?
It won't change who I am.
Can others accept it?
Can I accept them?
For we will meet each other eventually.
Just not sure if it will be peacefully.
We'll find out one day in our moment of passing...
Is it a dog fight, or a smile you see from me
As I fade out of sight.
I'm heading for the horizon...
The wild mustang in me flying!
Tires pounding!
So exciting!
Uncharted boundaries,
In my element.
My high is mounting,
The off beaten path calling!
Staking my own claim.
The new trail I've yet to name.
I could drive endlessly.
Forever you see...
But, the damn car needs gas!
Always something to stop my forward progress.
Guess I'll turn around and head back.
I've gone as far as I can today.
Still I smile inside;
For tomorrow is a new journey.
I smile again as I let out a sigh.
Content and fulfilled from my ride.
Happy inside.

DRIVING W/ ME

Today I stopped driving the Big Red Sled.
I hated it at first and rebelled, because it is so big.
It looks wider than any lane I'm in, and longer than sin.
I'm not good at driving things that are so big.
I don't like feeling intimidated.
I like to move and groove, run and jump;
But now I feel I'm in it for the long haul.
I think someone is trying to slow me up.
My stepson and my boyfriend sold my Mini-van.
I came back to the shop one day, they were washing it up.
Said it had been sold.
I said yea right,
They said... no doubt.
Then some people pulled up;
Went for a test drive — bought my car.
That's how I got stuck driving Big Red.
Already ours for quite a few years,
This gas hog was only used for hauling, here and there.
Now it is my every day car, my grip is tight.
I don't feel I fit in the lanes just right.
And the tinted cab windows
All the way down that just look black —
Well... I see my own reflection when I try to look back.
I can't see behind me at all, as a matter of fact.
It did slow me up for a while.
I stayed in my lane, drove just right.
But, I was on edge all the time, not feeling right.
Then one day I got stuck, behind 2 cars that kept slowing up.
The edgier I got — the slower they went.

Sitting right next to each other.
Neither of them... picking it up, or giving it up.
Both of them making sure of only one thing —
Keeping me behind them.
If so... their smile is a short lived thing.
I finally had it!
I floored it, and Big Red began to fly —
Off on the side of the road
And within seconds I passed them both by
Leaving them covered in a dust cloud.
That's when I first felt the power of this ride.
My fondness for it — grew wide.
If I was 1st in line —
I'd be gone when the light turned green.
The other cars still sitting there.
The light not yet registering.
And, for people going slow —
When a shadow over you this Big Red shows,
You know I am going to get in front of you on the road.
Wrong to say...
But like my big Parrot fish that passed away,
With Big Red, I was the intimidator, never intimidated.
I'm never scared with Big Red surrounding me.
And — my stepson Mike said to me recently...
Dad — We got to get the Honda running, and put Deb in it.
Deb — The Big Red sled is not a passing car,
It's a big   l — o — n — g   truck,
And you are jumping around in traffic
Like you've got a little Passat!
So relax Deb, chill out!

I'm driving fine I say.
It is not against the law to change lanes, and I always obey,
Using my turning signals effortlessly.
So — what if sometimes I don't have enough room;
I'm sure the other cars will realize, and compromise.
Just kidding I say.
I get 2 angry looks.
My sense of humor doesn't go over well,
Because they know me —
But, they don't see all of me.
Only when I am driving alone do I let myself really show.
Todd would never let me own a car if he knew
About the crazy driving that I often do.
But... they know enough to say,
Tomorrow the transmission goes back into the Honda,
And this is the car that I will drive away.

Don't get me wrong, the Honda is ok.
Any car I get may be slow to take off,
But within a few weeks of driving —
It will have learned to drive just like me.
I'm very strict in this rule,
And my cars learn fast to please me.

Now Big Red will again be sitting around,
Waiting to do the hauling;
While the Honda will be hauling ass with me.
And I am off again...
HAPPILY!

ABOUT THE AUTHOR

She was born and raised in Illinois.
From the time she was small,
Nature and adventure were kindred to her soul.
Growing up, she scared her parents, quite a lot.
She would disappear.
At 3 years old, with all the neighbors looking for her,
she was eventually found across a busy street, behind the
bowling alley, playing in a creek, trying to catch a frog.
She didn't understand why everyone was mad,
when she was so happy
They had to look for her qiute a lot.
By 6 years old she would make it deep into
The next town over before they found her.
Her parents would be furious, but her smile and laughter
almost always changed the atmosphere.
She could have happily grown up in the fields
with a sleeping bag.
She daydreamed in beautiful ways.
Poetic in her mind,
while she gently played with all the bugs.
As she got older,
her thoughts started coming to the forefront.
Her sensitivity made by nature captures the emotions of
others with words that come alive in her mind.
To this day, she is still the same way,
and to her longtime boyfriend's dismay...
He still keeps catching her –
Feeding a group of baby ants behind the shop;
Also back there is a chain link fence,

Where a flat bowl of water sits, and ripped up bread.
It's for the little birds that nest around there.
If a bee gets inside,
she'll catch him in a cup and return him to the outside.
Back at home, a skunk, an oppossum and a raccoon,
get their left over dinners.
She hides the food in the corner of the back yard,
so that no one but them will know.
The wild calico cat (Rainbow)
she feeds under the planted Land Rover in the driveway.
This freaks him out, but he loves her just the same;
and as she herself would say,
I'm just me, not a delectable flower,
but one of the cuter weeds in the field.
Lastly, they have been together for 15 years.
He is used to her by now, but yes, she still freaks him out.

The Ruins originally were built
With blood, sweat, and tears.
It was cruel.
It was gratifying.
It was pride and happiness.
It was heart and soul;
So as my book goes.
My poems have enriched people's lives.
I hope they do the same for you.
If not,
Do not despise;
But at least —
Try me on for size.

- Taxed
- Shorties Shorties Shorties Shorties
- Colic
- Simple Riches
- The Eyes Have It
- Young Love
- Loved Ones
- State Appeal
- Angels on Earth
- Illness
- Night & Day
- Dental Demise
- Self Worth
- A Darker Side
- Delivery
- My Best Friend
- Fish
- Driving w/ Me
- Addictions
- Bad Habits